Diary of a Currency Trader

A simple strategy for foreign exchange trading
and an illustration of it in practice over three
months in the market

By Samuel J. Rae

HARRIMAN HOUSE LTD

3A Penns Road
Petersfield
Hampshire
GU32 2EW
GREAT BRITAIN

Tel: +44 (0)1730 233870
Email: enquiries@harriman-house.com
Website: www.harriman-house.com

Published in Great Britain in 2013.
Copyright © Harriman House Ltd

The right of Samuel J. Rae to be identified as Author has been asserted in accordance with the Copyright, Designs and Patents Act 1988.

ISBN: 978-0-85719-338-4

British Library Cataloguing in Publication Data
A CIP catalogue record for this book can be obtained from the British Library.

No responsibility for loss occasioned to any person or corporate body acting or refraining to act as a result of reading material in this book can be accepted by the Publisher or by the Author.

 Harriman House

Contents

FREE EBOOK VERSION

As a buyer of the print book of *Diary of a Currency Trader* you can now download the eBook version free of charge to read on an eBook reader, your smartphone or your computer. Simply go to:

http://ebooks.harriman-house.com/currencytrader

or point your smartphone at the QRC below.

You can then register and download your free eBook.

FOLLOW US, LIKE US, EMAIL US

@HarrimanHouse
www.linkedin.com/company/harriman-house
www.facebook.com/harrimanhouse
contact@harriman-house.com

 Harriman House

About the author

Having completed his Economics BSc Degree in Manchester, Samuel J. Rae quickly discovered that the retail forex industry was for him. A short foray into the corporate world drove him to search for an alternative to the more traditional ways of making a living, and in becoming a retail trader he has achieved exactly that.

Through persistent market participation and extensive education he has grown to become a specialist in both fundamental and technical analysis.

His personal trading style combines classic candlestick analysis with a simple, logical and risk management driven approach to the financial markets – a strategy that is described and demonstrated in his *Diary of a Currency Trader*.

Preface

I'd like to be clear from the start. This book is not a beginner's guide to foreign exchange or a how-to manual that will tell you how to follow a definite strategy. There are countless other books and online resources available that explain the basics of forex trading, or claim to present a system that guarantees profitability. This is not one of them. This book is for anyone who wants to know exactly how one trader operates and profits in the foreign exchange market.

As such, if you are new to forex and you are not familiar with the way the market or individual trades work, down to such terms as pips and pairs, then I recommend you read up on this first. Similarly, my method employs candlestick charts and basic technical analysis. If you are not familiar with these concepts then you will need to obtain this knowledge before you read on. I have included a 'Useful resources' section at the end of the book in which I suggest where you can start.

There are many different ways to achieve success in the currency markets and my approach is just an example. It should be taken as such. Rather than try to convince anyone that they should follow my methods, I want this book to show the concepts and the principles I apply to my trading. Risk management, trading psychology and constant self-assessment are qualities that very few unsuccessful traders possess, and all successful traders share. Developing these qualities is much more important than learning how to use a particular indicator, or having a feel for what combination of signals implies entry.

In order to give a complete and unaltered insight into my trading life I have structured this book in the form of a diary. The first half of the book lays out my strategy; from my risk management principles, to how I think and feel about trading, to what patterns I use the most and why. The second half covers three months of my own personal trading; every trade, win or lose, and my reasoning for and reaction to each. Before I wrote the book I had no idea how the three months of trading would turn out and my analysis is presented as it was performed.

At the end of the book, along with the list of recommended resources, is an appendix with charts showing the price activity of three currency pairs in 2011. I make reference to these charts in my trading diary.

Introduction

One thing that always interests me is how other people trade. Be it stocks, options or currencies, everyone has their own style, methods and approach. It amazes me what sparse literature is available that covers these things in any depth and this is my attempt to redress the balance.

If you have spent any amount of time immersed in the trading world, or perhaps even if you haven't, you will have seen a huge number of books titled *This Winning Strategy*, or *That Winning Strategy*. I myself have probably read 20 different books of this type, under different guises, and at the end of each one I am always left thinking, "Well, show me then!" Having written *Diary of a Currency Trader*, I now know why many authors choose to *tell* people about their strategy but not *show* it in action.

If I'm being honest, when I sat down to write this book I had no idea what I was getting into. The trading itself was of course normal to me. The reflection on each trade, again, was normal. Putting it all down on paper in a way that somebody else might understand, on the other hand, was not something I was accustomed to.

A strategy that you follow every day can seem relatively simple in your head, but when it comes to deconstructing it and presenting it to someone else it ceases to be so. On top of this, sitting at your computer and writing about your winners is an enjoyable task, but doing the same with your losers is not.

I also had to work hard not to let the thought that I was going to be writing my diary each evening affect my trading decisions. One of the things I talk about a little later on in the book is how you shouldn't let the outcome of one trade influence another, but this is a very difficult thing to do if after a string of losers you know you will be sitting down and dissecting the trades, writing them up for others to read about!

Anyway, I got through it, and this is the finished piece. My aim was to write a book that would illustrate what it is like to trade, and what one particular trader goes through on a daily basis. I think I have succeeded.

If you take just one thing away with you I hope it's that retail foreign exchange trading is difficult and emotionally taxing, but doable. You do not need God-given talent, nor do you need expensive mentorship or sophisticated computer programs. With the availability of mini lot trading you don't even need vast capital resources. All you need is time, hard work and a sound grasp of risk management principles. In reverse order.

Enjoy.

Chapter One

Birth of a Trader

This chapter looks at me as a trader: how I first got interested in the world of currency trading, where it took me and ultimately how I came to the point I am at today.

I have to start with something of an apology though. I imagine most of you have picked up this book intending to really dig deep into the mechanics of trading foreign currencies for a living. You've finally found some time to sit down and get stuck in, and here, right at the opening turn, I am first going to subject you to a history lesson.

Here's the good news. This history section is what you might call a small liberty of mine. It is only short. The history of currencies, their birth and life cycle, are a sort of private infatuation for me. From the ancient introduction of coins as a means of value storage, through to the modern day reserve strength of the US dollar, the journey that money has made over the past few thousand years fascinates me, but it often escapes the interest of the general audience. If I mention the Bretton Woods agreement to others I know who are interested in trading, it is as if I have started a race for the door.

What I have found over the years is that traders often develop an intrigue for the history of currencies once they have started to make money and so, for those of you who are not yet looking to dwell on the past, I will forgive you for skipping this section. You will not miss anything especially important, or ground-breaking.

All I ask is that once you have read the rest, give this section a try. One thing that history often affords us is perspective, and whilst this may not be key to your strategy when operating in the market, as you will read, it is key to mine.

A SHORT HISTORY LESSON

Origins of the world's biggest market

Take a look at the foreign exchange market today, with all its many bells and whistles, and you could be forgiven for thinking that any semblance of comparison with early exchange systems or coinage uses would be useless. And you would be right, partly.

Somewhere between two and a half and three thousand years ago, our ancestors of the ancient world lived life with a focus on many of the same fundamentals as we do today. Food, sleep, work, play and faith were the areas of life that demanded the most attention, with sleep necessary for work, work allowing people to eat and faith keeping play in check!

Individuals would farm crops, or raise cattle, which would then be traded at market. For example, if an ancient Egyptian cattle farmer needed wheat for his bread, he would march one of his cows to market and trade that cow for its proportionate value in wheat. Now the cow farmer has wheat, the wheat farmer has meat and milk, and everyone is happy.

The problem comes when the cattle farmer needs some bread, but the wheat farmer already has enough meat and milk. The cattle farmer in this case could find a commodity the wheat farmer needs, say firewood, trade his cattle with the woodcutter for firewood, then trade the firewood for wheat. Simple enough you say? Well, what if neither the woodcutter nor the wheat farmer need cattle?

In this example, where there are three goods to be traded, and three individuals with differing needs, the laws of supply and demand suggest that the value of the cattle is zero, as neither the wheat farmer nor the woodcutter need meat. Of course, this is not the case. More accurately, the value of the cattle *at this time* is zero. However when the woodcutter's family have eaten all their meat, the demand will increase to meet the level of supply. In other words, *equilibrium* has been reached in the market.

What is needed to ensure the smooth running of this system is some form of storage mechanism; a token that represents the intrinsic value of a good and has the same representation today as it will tomorrow. With this store of value, the cattle farmer can buy wheat, regardless of whether the wheat farmer needs cattle today, tomorrow, or next year. All he needs to do when he does want to buy is take that value store back to the cattle farmer and it can be traded for cattle.

Emergence of coins

This token storage mechanism became known as the coin. When a monetary system of exchange was first employed, the coins that were being produced were invariably fixed weights of gold or silver, used to represent predetermined amounts of tradable goods. The first fixed gold representation is believed to have been produced by the Trojans – a gold piece coined with the head of an ox. It represented a fixed amount of oxen and could be traded as such.

After this specific representation came a more generalised coinage system. In place of the goods traded, the ox in this example, a representation of the nation of origin would be coined on to gold – a somewhat closer relation to the coins we use today.

With the expansion of ancient empires came an ever-increasing requirement for international trade. This caused problems in that one nation's coinage was not valid under another's rule, and so some mechanism through which natively coined gold and silver could be traded for the foreign equivalent was required. This mechanism came in the form of money changers who would set up stalls, often in temples, and offer rates at which a currency could be swapped.

These money changers would take an interest payment as commission, a practice which is often referenced as unholy or illegal in the *Bible* and other writings of the time, as under Jewish financial law the charging of interest is illegal. A topic worthy of a book in itself, this illegality, referred to in the book of Ezekiel as being "among the worst of sins", remains today, however the Jewish financial community have developed ways around it to accommodate modern day financial practice.

Foreign exchange practices were expanded greatly in the fourteenth and fifteenth centuries by the Medici Family, a political dynasty which created the Medici Bank. The Medici Bank was one of the largest and most respected banks in Europe, and quickly became known as a hub for exchanging and holding foreign currencies throughout the continent. As part of their operations, they opened various institutions across Europe to facilitate international trade.

Modern systems of currency exchange

This system soon became obsolete, with the expansion of international trade fuelled by the ever-growing British Empire requiring larger and larger amounts of currency to be carried. This was overcome by introducing bills of exchange, which were representative of a certain amount of a nation's currency. In the 1800s, the gold standard was introduced, which fixed a country's bill of exchange to gold reserves, reinforcing the validity of the medium.

The gold standard ran unopposed until the outbreak of war in 1914. Fuelled by a protectionist approach to international trade and then the meltdown of the world's financial system that led to the Great Depression, the Bretton Woods framework was proposed and agreed in 1944. This framework tied its signatories to a pegging of their currencies to the US dollar by means of an exchange rate and served to stabilise the foreign exchange market for a further 30 years.

In 1971, however, the exchangeability of currency for US gold was causing serious problems for the UK and other nations, and the system was dropped and replaced with the Smithsonian Agreement. This system allowed for much more flexibility in the fluctuation of currency values, but again ran into trouble and in early 1973 was dropped and replaced with the free floating exchange system we have today.

Under the free floating exchange rate system a currency's value is not linked directly to any amount of gold or silver. It is merely a token of exchange, supported by goodwill alone. What this means is that those notes in your pocket have no intrinsic value whatsoever. They rely solely on the goodwill of the person with whom you wish to trade in terms of defining their value.

This potted history brings us pretty much up to the present day, the only major change over the past 30 years being the introduction of the internet, which has brought a vast amount of activity from currency traders and speculators, like me and you, who otherwise would not be able to operate in such a market.

AN OBSESSION SPARKED

Mention the words *foreign exchange trading* amongst a group of unsuspecting individuals and you will receive a mixed response. For some, the thought of currency trading evokes visions of wealth, pleasure and free time. These are the people that will listen to what you have to say, but are more interested in what trading affords you than what it involves.

For others, foreign exchange trading is a form of gambling, a speculative road to financial ruin. Whether gained through tall tales or personal experience, this perception of trading is a very hard one to change; one that I have personally spent many hours fighting to overturn, with limited success.

For a select few, however, the mention of the market can be all it takes to fuel evenings full of musings, strategy comparison and predictive thought. These are the people that I hope you, as readers, already are, or will become; those with a genuine passion for the markets, not solely as a money-making tool, but as a way of life. This is how I like to view the markets, a view that I think is key to success.

First foray into investing

My personal trading life started whilst I was an economics undergraduate. Before any of you without a degree in economics become disheartened, I will point out that although it helped me develop an understanding of the dynamics of the markets, and the way in which certain macroeconomic events may have an effect on currencies, the majority of what I learnt I have never put to any sort of practical use. Any suggestion that you need some form of formal qualification to become a trader is incorrect. I just happened to be studying an economics degree at the time my interest in the markets was sparked.

About halfway through my first year of study, one of my lecturers presented the class with a challenge. The task was a simple one. Using a demo account, select and purchase a number of stocks, based upon whatever criteria we saw fit, and hold them. At the end of the semester, we would present our choices to the class, justify them, and evaluate the results. My journey had begun.

I started out by studying the earnings reports of a number of stocks. Thinking I was Ben Graham II, I used what I felt was a foolproof method to *value* a selection of stocks, much of which can be found in Mr Graham's wonderful book, *The Intelligent Investor*.

I bought those which I felt were most undervalued, and waited. Invariably, when it came to presenting and justifying our selections, the vast majority of us had lost huge sums of virtual money. I, for example, had committed the cardinal sin of not taking time into consideration. The method I had used to label my selections as undervalued required much more time than I had available for the stocks to turn from undervalued to reflecting true value, so many of my stocks had fallen or remained where they were when I bought them.

Quite amazingly, this crushing (imaginary) financial loss had done nothing to dampen my intrigue. Quite the opposite. The excitement I had experienced when it came to checking my results and throughout the period over which I held my portfolio was one I had not felt before and one that still has never been rivalled to this day, other than in my currency trading operations.

As a side note, although I have never been a big gambler myself, I think this excitement is comparable to that feeling whilst waiting for the roulette wheel to stop, or in deciding whether to stick or hit in blackjack, and the comparisons with gambling are born from this thrill. This is where the comparison stops, however. As you will read a little later on, with currency trading we have the ability to stack the deck in our favour, or tilt the wheel so as to maintain the excitement but massively reduce the uncertainty.

Anyway, this flutter into the world of speculation was all it took to spark within me a lifelong obsession with the markets and, more specifically, profiting from them.

Trading career

My trading career started with the stock market. Although I was aware the foreign exchange market existed, it was another world to me. With a company's stock, although there are a number of external factors that cannot be measured, the core of any business can be quantified.

Say, for example, you wanted to know whether stocks in a company are correctly priced. You can look at the financial reports and from these ascertain whether the current share price is a true representation of the intrinsic value of a company's assets and earnings capability. If your analysis suggested the stock was cheap you would buy, hold and, if correct, you would sell at a profit once the share price had risen. The same, of course, applies in reverse.

I used this method in what I call an *inactive* way. By this I mean that I was looking for stocks that would generate profits over the long term; stocks that I could buy and forget about, whilst my analysis was proven correct or incorrect. With this method of stock market operating I made and lost small amounts of money here and there. Never enough to fund the lifestyle I was leading but more than enough to hold my interest in the field. It was only after my introduction to the benefits of trading in the foreign exchange market that the possibility of trading as a profession presented itself as realistic to me.

At this time I was working in a trainee advisory role at a small portfolio management company. Most of my working day was spent on the phone to clients, persuading them that we knew exactly what was about to happen in the market, when really we had no idea. I would also share tips and suggestions with others who were involved in the markets themselves. Although I would very rarely follow any of these tips I would always be intrigued about the story behind them – stories that would often lead to heated debates as to their authenticity.

One such debate was sparked when a colleague suggested I have a look at a particular currency pair. I forget which one, but he figured it was due for a big kick in the coming few days. I ask you to remember that, at this point, my knowledge of the foreign exchange market was limited to what I had picked up from others. I knew of the market, I knew it was traded in heavily by governments and large banking organisations, and I also knew that entering into this market would pitch me against them in my quest for profit.

What I did not know was the huge liquidity this organisational trading afforded the markets, and in turn, the freedom this liquidity gave individual retail traders when it came to buying and selling decisions, and risk management. The kick my colleague expected was based on the fact that the pair had broken out of its trading range, reversed, and what was previously acting as the top of the range was now offering support.

At the time I believed technical analysis in this manner was ridiculous and denounced the prediction. The debate raged, but in the event the support held and the bragging rights belonged to my colleague. I was forced to concede that there may be something in technical foreign exchange trading and decided that I would take a look at it. The rest, as they say, is history.

Currencies

From this moment on, my speculative endeavours invariably involved currency pairs. It was like a whole new world had opened up to me. Online foreign exchange brokering systems were beginning to take hold of the retail forex market and the panoply of tools, applications and techniques that were at my disposal changed foreign exchange trading from something of an unpredictable alternative to stock trading to a secure, information-rich environment in which I could speculate at will. Or so I thought.

I utter these words as a cautionary tale. As I am sure you are all aware, there is a vast amount of information available at the click of a mouse as to the future movements of currency pairs, and the possible causes of these movements. There are many that claim to be able to use this information to calculate exactly where the market will move next and how to profit from that movement. There are many too that claim to be able to code this analysis as software, which will trade on your behalf, resulting in guaranteed profits.

For starters, this is nonsense. Anybody who tells you they know for sure where a market will go is either ignorant or lying. What many people don't realise is that, especially in modern times, almost every possible bit of information that could possibly affect the price of one currency against another has already been accounted for in the quoted price. The speed with which information travels is much faster than the speed at which it used to in the past and with this change comes a required change in operating methods within the market.

I will cover this in more detail later on, but just to give you an example, say for argument's sake that it is the late 1920s and a stock operator in London has a brother who manages construction projects in Japan. One evening, after the market closes and just before the London investor turns in for the night, he receives a telegram from his brother to say that in the last hour there has been a terrible earthquake and much infrastructure has been destroyed. Over the course of the next few hours this information would slowly travel across the world, filtering through to businesses and governments by morning.

For a stock operator in these times, this is a window of opportunity. There are many ways in which a savvy operator could profit from this catastrophe. One such method would be to short sell the large insurance organisations in Japan, or to short the large UK-based investment houses with a stake in construction projects in Japan. By the time the bell goes the next morning, the operator can be set to sell these stocks, and as their value tumbles as the information trickles in, he can take his profits.

This is an example of what I like to call *information arbitrage*. Although this is a crude example of how it was used, it was a popular method of market operation many years ago. Nowadays, however, whilst these gaps in information do still occur, they are much harder to find, and much less substantial when you do find them.

This is just one instance where a method that might have worked in the past is no longer as effective due to changes in the mechanics of trading. What was once the key to making money – information – is now taken as a given and other ways to garner an advantage must be sought. The method I have developed, the method I use to this day and present to you in this book, is one such way of garnering said advantage.

HONING MY CRAFT

The proverb *practice makes perfect* is believed to have originated somewhere in rural England around the middle ages. Since then it has become one of the most widely used ways to illustrate the idea that if you do something over and over again, at some point you will become great at it. There are many instances in which this is true: a concert pianist may repeat the same bars of a concerto until he can play them with his eyes closed; a competitive swimmer might try and perfect her launch off by diving into a pool many times; or a basketball star might practise his free-throw until he never misses. You get the idea. A slightly less well known reincarnation of this phrase was quoted by Henry Longhurst, a respected golf writer and former MP. He stated (with regard to golfing), that "Practice does not make perfect, it merely consolidates imperfection."

I came to realise that in trading, both of these statements are true. Whether or not success is reached is not rooted in the act of practice, of repetition, but in the direction in which that practice is focused. What I mean by this is that it is not enough to work and work at something if that something fails to produce a desired outcome. In trading terms, there is no point in developing and implementing a strategy that does not create long-term gains in a market. Many traders think they have found their golden strategy when a string of winners comes along only to find that over the long term their strategy is ineffective.

The first thing I should say is that while I have alluded to my stock buying experiences, they should not be compared with the way I operate in the foreign exchange market. My stock operations were based upon quantitative analysis and executed as buy-and-hold, for months, even years, at a time.

The way in which I operate in the currency markets is much shorter term and the only bit of information I use when it comes to identifying my trades is *price action*. To my mind, price action is pure and simple price movement. The direction in which price moves, how it gets from point A to point B, and the time it takes to do so. As I've already mentioned, in such a fast-paced world as foreign currency trading, every other bit of information has already been built into the price, so why would I look at anything else?

Another stark difference is in the way I actually analyse my trade opportunities. With stock trading, I would pore over earnings reports and other financial data with the hope of finding a *cheap* stock. This quantitative analysis is replaced in my forex trading by technical analysis.

It is neither my wish nor my intention for this book to be a forex education for beginners, so if you are unfamiliar with the notion of technical analysis, or *charting* as it is also referred to, then it is worth doing some research before you proceed. You will stand a much higher chance of successfully putting the practices outlined in this book into action if you familiarise yourself with the basics of the vast topic of technical analysis. Suggested resources can be found at the end of the book.

Technical analysis

In a nutshell, technical analysis involves plotting price on a chart, giving a visual representation of price movements over a certain period of time. This visual representation enables the trader to recognise at a glance levels at which price has encountered reversals in the past. When price returns to these levels, we can expect either the predefined levels to hold, or not. It is the price action around these levels that can give us clues as to which of the two paths price is likely to follow.

Often price will form patterns at these levels that are repeated throughout historical data, so the rules I follow state that if a recognisable pattern has developed in a currency pair, at a predefined price level where a similar pattern has developed before, then I consider the trade. Of course, whether I actually take the trade is based upon other factors too, including the risk-reward available, and I will go into this in much more detail in the next section. But in its purest form, that is all my strategy involves.

The real challenge comes in being able to weed out those patterns that indicate some form of predictable movement and those that don't. Over hundreds and hundreds of trades, and many hours of what I call *screen time*, I came to the conclusion that longer-term gains become much more likely through the use of a small number of high probability patterns (setups) than through use of a higher number of less reliable setups. Although fewer opportunities were presented, if I could develop a strategy that would take full advantage of those that I felt were high probability, then over the long term I would surely benefit.

So this is what I did. I developed a method of operating in the market that identifies high probability price action setups, forming around historically important price levels. In the next chapter I will explain my methods in detail.

Chapter Two

The Way I Trade

In this chapter I explain how I trade using the tools and components of my trading plan, and how I put this into practice in my trading strategy.

MY TRADING PLAN

There are four components to my trading plan, which I will describe in turn here:

1. Charts
2. Candlesticks
3. Historic price levels
4. Timing

1. Charts

When explaining how I trade, the natural starting point is my use of charts. As I have mentioned, charts are a graphical representation of historical price data. This graphical representation makes it much easier to locate points at which there has previously been price contention and it can also offer an indication of the direction in which a market is heading and the strength associated with future moves. Charting can be extremely useful – indeed I would not be able to trade the way I do without it – but you must be very careful in your interpretation of charts in order to benefit from them.

Time frame

One key characteristic of a chart is its time frame. That is whether the chart represents months, weeks, days, hours or minutes of price action data.

My preference is to use daily charts. This means that each bar on the chart represents one day of price action. This makes it possible to effectively view price action over periods of three to six months on a single chart on a computer screen. I use the word *effectively*, as it is possible to use a daily chart to view years of price action if you want to, but specific levels are much harder to detect on one graph over such a long period.

It suits my strategy to consider three to six months of action on a single chart as I have found that over this period of time historical price levels are more reliable. This is as opposed to shorter periods where historical price levels are less reliable and longer periods where the price levels are more obscure and they are more difficult to spot.

For example, if price has reversed at a certain point twice over a period of six months, one could deduce that there is a good chance of price reversing again at this point, when it is reached. Even if it does not reverse the next time it gets to that level, you could at least expect some strong movement. Conversely, if the chart you are looking at represents six hours of data and price has reversed at the same level twice over the period, the probability of a further reversal is much less.

This principle of price repeatedly respecting a previous level is illustrated in Figure 2.1 – you can see that price reverses at around 1.4567 three times in the period from June to August 2011. Please be mindful that this chart is for illustration purposes only and although it represents what happens a higher proportion of the time, I could just as easily find an example where price did not respect historic levels.

FIGURE 2.1 – DAILY CHART SHOWING PRICE RESPECTING HISTORIC LEVELS

Clean charts

I consider the use of *clean* charts to be key to successful technical analysis.

I am sure that if you are reading this book, you will have had some exposure to the vast amount of indicators, oscillators and chart notation that is available to help inform your trading decisions. Whilst many traders seem to use these tools, it is worth remembering that over years of use, no single indicator has been developed that consistently produces gains in the currency market.

Indicators are often marketed as foolproof signals that will tell you when to enter and exit trades, but when considered for what they actually are, the sheer amount of people who swear by them never ceases to amaze me.

Every single indicator in existence, from RSI to MACD to a simple moving average, is derived from previous price action. More often than not, closing prices are taken from a set number of periods, depending upon the time frames you are considering, and manipulated to form a moving average whose properties change depending upon the movement over that period. What's more, this moving average lags behind price action, in that its movement trails that of price. This lag often means that the movement the moving average indicates has already taken place, or is already taking place, by the time the indication is made.

I hear you ask – *Surely this just produces a line that shows how price has moved in the past?* Correct.

But do we not already have that – a line that graphically represents the movement of price in the past? Correct.

So is it not logical to conclude that out of the two lines I have available to me, it would be better to rely on the actual representation of price now, rather than a lagging representation of previous price action? Yes!

Two versions of the same chart are illustrated in Figures 2.2 and 2.3, one with a number of the more popular indicators included (MACD, RSI, Bollinger Bands and a simple moving average, as labelled), one clean.

Consider this. When looking at these two charts with the primary goal of identifying levels at which price has reversed in the past, do the indicators help or do they confuse and clutter things? My personal opinion is very firmly the latter.

FIGURE 2.2 – CHART WITH SOME OF THE MORE POPULAR INDICATORS

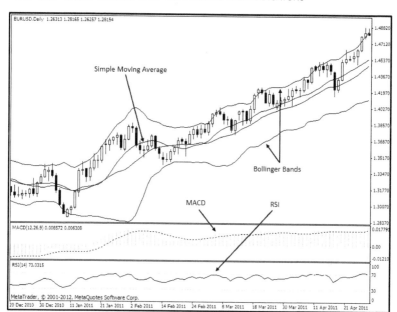

FIGURE 2.3 – THE SAME CHART, WITHOUT INDICATORS

A small caveat should be noted to my unprovoked abuse of indicators. Whilst I find no utility in using indicators to predict future price movements, certain ones can make it easier to identify trends. For example, I often use a simple moving average to help me determine my directional bias. More on this later.

2. Candlesticks

I have explained how I use daily charts of price movement to represent where price has moved over a period of time. It is now important for me to explain how I like to see price movements represented on the chart.

There are a number of representations of how price has moved, with my preference being the use of candlesticks. Candlesticks, a Japanese method that was first introduced to Western chartists by Steve Nison in the early 1990s, illustrate the open, close, high and low of price during a particular session. *Session* refers to the time period of the candlestick – it could be a minute, a day, a week or a month of trading. So, for example, a daily candlestick will show where price opened that day, where it closed, and what prices its high and low reached.

An example of a classic bullish candlestick can be seen in Figure 2.4. Here, you can see the market closed higher than it opened and you can also see the high and low of the day. The main body of the candlestick shows the opening and closing prices, and the thin line that extends above and below the main body – known as the *wick* or the *tail* of the candlestick – illustrates the high and low prices of the day.

FIGURE 2.4 - A CLASSIC BULLISH CANDLESTICK

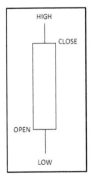

Indicators of directional bias

The beauty of candlesticks, and the reason I use them over other methods such as bar charts, is their simplicity. At a glance it is possible to gain a real insight into the important levels of a period and also the movement within these levels – the open, close, high and low points of the period in question. It is this knowledge of movement that helps me form a bias about the possible future direction of a currency pair.

Every trader will have their own preference as to the format of their candlesticks, but generally for a session during which price increased (opened lower than it closed) the body of the candlestick will be coloured green, blue or white and for a session during which price decreased (closed lower than it opened) the body of the candlestick will be coloured red or black. In my own charting I prefer to use white for an up-candle and black for a down-candle.

For example, in the session illustrated by the candlestick in Figure 2.5 (which is a classic bullish pin candlestick), we can see that price opened and closed at similar levels. The candlestick is white, which tells us the opening price of the session was lower than the closing price – this was an up day. We can also see that at some point between these levels price dropped substantially (as indicated by the long lower wick), but returned to just above its opening level before the session closed.

FIGURE 2.5 – A CLASSIC BULLISH PIN CANDLESTICK

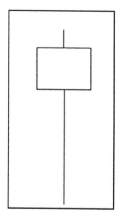

What does this candlestick tell me?

The fact that price opened and closed at a similar level suggests that there exists an element of uncertainty in the market, which once overcome could lead to a substantial movement in price. I also deduce that since price fell and then returned to its former levels within a session, there must be considerable buying pressure below the open and close levels. From this information alone, it is logical to conclude that the market in question could be due for a movement upwards, built upon this buying pressure.

Of course, the bullish pin candlestick is just one of many that can be used to form a bias as to the possible future direction of price. I have used it as an example because it is one of my favourites; other traders will have their own favourites. If you want to find out more on the topic of candlestick anatomy and different types of candlesticks there is a wealth of information available. See the 'Useful resources' section for some sources I would recommend.

Candlestick patterns

Whilst it is possible to trade using single candlestick formations such as the pin bar, further advantage can be gained when groups of candlesticks form patterns. Such patterns can be strong indicators of a directional bias and with a little bit of practice these can become very simple to identify and act upon.

There are a huge number of patterns available and just as with individual candlesticks traders will have their own personal favourites. I trade only a small number of patterns that I deem to be the most reliable on the timeframes I use and in the way that I trade them. These are described a little later on in the book. It is important to realise that while I limit the number of patterns I use because it suits my strategy and risk tolerance, you should not feel restricted to the same limitations.

To illustrate the concept of trading with candlestick patterns, I will use one that I trade regularly; the *inside candle*. Inside candles are formed when one session's price action is completely engulfed by the price action in the previous session. This is illustrated in Figure 2.6.

FIGURE 2.6 – INSIDE DAY CANDLESTICK

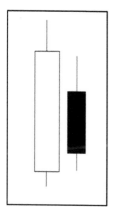

What does this pattern tell me?

I can see that during the inside session, price was unable to reach either the high or the low of the previous day. This, in much the same way as a pin bar, indicates a level of uncertainty and consolidation in the market. I like to think of the inside session as the spring that fuels the movement of price being coiled. This simple analogy reminds me that when price does start to move it will continue to do so and therefore once movement does take place a trade can be entered.

It is worth noting that inside candles alone are not what I trade – it is the subsequent break of the engulfing bar after the pattern has been seen that indicates entry. Finer details such as entry and risk parameters will be covered in 'My favourite setups'.

Risk management with candlesticks

It is possible to use the levels indicated by a candlestick to set risk management parameters. I have a whole chapter on risk management so for now I will say that the highs and lows indicated by a candlestick's wick are often the points at which any directional bias gleaned becomes invalid.

So, for example, looking at Figure 2.5, if price were to fall below the low of this session (the lower wick extreme) in the next session then my suggestion that there was enough buying pressure to hold price above this low would be proved wrong. The basis on which I entered the trade would thus be incorrect and so I would not want to be in the trade. Accordingly, if I had entered a long trade in the session that followed this candlestick, the low of the bullish pin is the point at which I would have placed my stop loss.

3. Historic price levels

Now I have shown how candlesticks represent price movement over a period of time and I have illustrated the concept of using candlesticks and the patterns they form to get a sense of possible future price direction, we must look at where we would expect these patterns to form and what sort of movements they indicate. This key insight can be gleaned from studying previous price action.

Regardless of what any trader tells you and however much work they claim to have put into developing their infallible strategy, each and every one of us parts with our money on a very simple assumption: that what has gone before will come again. More succinctly, where price action has occurred in the past, we have to assume it will happen again and it will happen in a similar way.

This assumption will not be accurate in every case – many times I have watched price soar through a level at which it had previously reversed and vice versa – but analysis of past price action and projection of patterns into the future is how traders gain their competitive edge in the market.

Patterns won't repeat in the same way every time but a key point to remember – and one that I will cover in more detail in the psychology section of this book – is that not every trade is going to be a winner. *Obvious*, I hear you say? Well, in a sense, but consider this: if I know and accept that I will have losing trades in advance, then why should I be disappointed when I make a losing trade? If I have a reliable long-term strategy, then surely each losing trade I make increases the odds that the next trade will be a winner? A certain level of detachment like this is required to enable traders to execute strategies correctly and by achieving this detachment it becomes much more likely that strategies will produce positive longer-term results.

The way in which I use historic price levels is by observing support and resistance.

Support and resistance

If price reverses to the downside more than once at a similar level, that level is referred to as *resistance*. Conversely, if price reverses to the upside more than once at a similar level, that level is referred to as *support*.

To illustrate the power of support and resistance price levels in predicting future movements, in Figure 2.7 I present a daily chart spanning six months of EUR/USD price action.

FIGURE 2.7 – HISTORIC PRICES INITIATING REVERSALS IN EUR/USD

As you can see in the chart, price rose to around 1.4535 in early July, then reversed and took a substantial drop of about 600 pips. About a week after peaking, price bottomed at just below 1.4000 and started to pick up again.

The rise was a little slower than the fall but sure enough after nearly two weeks price approached its previous high at 1.4535. What did it do when it reached that level? It did exactly the same as it had a few weeks earlier; it turned and reversed!

Now, I should say that in hindsight it is easy to look at a chart and pick out points at which the market did as you would expect it to, so although price had reversed at this level recently, for some traders this alone might not be enough to warrant action. What I would have picked up in live trading is the apparent importance of this level and I would make a note to observe future price action at this level.

Having marked this resistance level as one to watch, I wait. The ability to wait is another often overlooked, but key, trait that every trader must develop. I wait until price starts to head towards the level I have highlighted and then I watch. As you can see in Figure 2.8 – zoomed in to the relevant section of the chart – sure enough price reached 1.4535, in this instance slightly higher, but was not able to close above it and in due course reversed. On this occasion it never looked back.

FIGURE 2.8 – PRICE HITTING SLIGHTLY HIGHER THAN 1.4535 IN EUR/USD

So how would I trade this?

Having identified the key historic price levels, I would wait for a tell-tale sign that history was going to repeat. This tell-tale sign comes from price action, illustrated through candlesticks. As you can see, towards the end of August, a bearish pin bar formed, with the wick breaking, but the session not closing above, the previous two highs.

This indicates to me that although during the session of the bearish pin bar the price rose above 1.4535, it was not able to close above this level due to selling pressure in this area. As mentioned earlier, when I see a pin bar candlestick I use this to help me form a directional bias for my trade. In this case, the combination of the resistance level holding once again and the bearish pin bar would have triggered a short entry for me, with my stop loss set at the high of the pin bar and entry at the open of the following candle.

Trend channels

This basic concept of history repeating itself in the form of recurring price patterns can be applied to many different strategy shapes and sizes. Some traders prefer trend channels, for example, rather than horizontal levels of support and resistance.

A trend channel forms when price trends upwards or downwards between diagonal upper and lower channel lines, the upper channel line acting as resistance and the lower channel line acting as support. An example trend channel can be seen in Figure 2.9.

FIGURE 2.9 – A TREND CHANNEL IN EUR/USD

Personally I use trend channels much less than simple support and resistance as I feel a trend channel can cloud judgment. Also, it can suggest a continuing trend when, by the time the channel is recognisable, the trend is reversing. But this is not to say trend channels have no use. No two traders are identical and no two traders use identical methods so you might find channels work better for your method.

4. Timing

By timing, I mean the time at which I analyse the market and place my trades.

Most of my trades are taken at what is referred to as New York close; this is 5pm EST. The forex market is open 24 hours a day and as such there are no natural opening and closing times for daily candlesticks. As a result, it is necessary to line up the candlesticks with the times that reflect the most accurate representation of the day's trading activity.

The forex market is unofficially split into three main sessions, each of which is based around the banking hours of the three major financial continents: Europe, Asia and North America. The close of the North American session is at 5pm EST (as New York banks close for the day at this time) and the opening of the Asian session (as Sydney banks open for the day). I find in my own trading that by basing my analysis (and my trades) on this particular reference point in the day I get the best results. In the diary, you will see that most of my analysis is made on the charts as they are at the New York close.

MY TRADING STRATEGY

Having outlined the three components of my trading plan – charts, candlesticks and historic price levels – I will now show how these components fit together to form my trading strategy.

I will also explain how and why risk management is a vital part of my strategy.

Candlestick formations and historic price levels

I begin by considering recent price action. I mark the key swing points over a minimum of the last three months on a daily chart and look to see if price is approaching any of these levels. This first step is illustrated in Figure 2.10 for EUR/USD in the period December 2010 to April 2011.

FIGURE 2.10 – EUR/USD DAILY CHART WITH KEY SWING POINTS

There is no real science to identifying the key levels, they can just be any recent highs or lows that have turned price around. They can be marked as resistance, i.e. recent highs, or support, i.e. recent lows.

If, as above, price is heading towards a level I have marked as important I zoom into a chart's price action over the past month or two. This enables me to get a closer look at the price patterns that are forming. Figure 2.11 shows the section of the chart I would zoom in on as price approaches the previous resistance level.

FIGURE 2.11 – PRICE APPROACHING A KEY HISTORIC RESISTANCE LEVEL IN EUR/USD

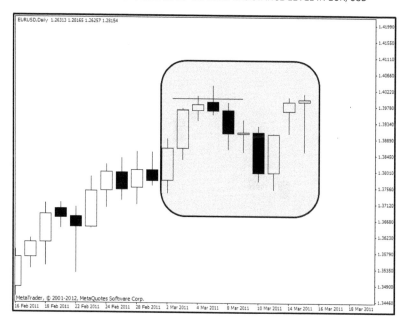

This is one of those moments where waiting is key. Consider this. What are the chances that the moment I chose to turn on my computer, load up my trading platform, analyse the chart of my choice and form a bias in terms of direction, is the best moment to implement that bias and execute a trade? *Very small.*

I must wait until I get a sign that the movement in the direction in which I have laid my bias is about to happen. This sign comes from the candlesticks. I discuss the entry signals of a few of my favourite setups in the next section, but for illustration's sake, when I trade a pin bar candlestick I wait until the session closes. If the candlestick is still a pin bar at session close then I consider my bias confirmed.

Again, purely for the sake of illustration, Figure 2.12 shows where price moved after this pin bar candlestick closed.

FIGURE 2.12 – THE SAME EUR/USD DAILY CHART, REVEALING PRICE ACTION THAT
DEVELOPED AFTER THE PIN BAR CANDLESTICK IN QUESTION

Figure 2.13, a new chart example, shows price forming a number of key lows, without making any new highs, indicating that there is a downward trend in progress. A closer look tells me that price has recently made a new low and has turned upwards correctively.

FIGURE 2.13 – SHORT-TERM CORRECTION AGAINST THE TREND '

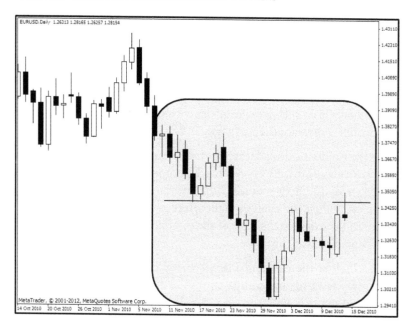

Since I am assuming a downtrend, this correction is traders booking sell profits, or covering buy losses, rather than overwhelming buying pressure. So I assume that at some point the price will again turn and the downtrend will continue.

What price do I look to as being that likely turning point? In this instance, I look at the previous swing low in early December. As price approached the resistance level at which the previous swing low began for the second time, I can see that a pin bar formed, up and through the resistance level, but the market was not able to close above it. This is a major sign that the level will hold.

So do I place a trade?

Not yet. First I must look at the risk-reward scenario available to me. I do this by calculating how far price is likely to fall once it turns downward at the resistance level and thus setting my profit target. I personally like to use two levels in my placement of a profit target. The first of these is at the recent swing low, which is a support level from which price rebounded. Assuming a downtrend, I would expect price to fall to at least this point again. In the example this support is around 1.2960.

The second profit target I like to use, if available, is a key level at which price has found support or resistance before. This is for use in trades where I feel the downtrend is a strong one and a large movement is likely. There is no such level immediately identifiable in Figure 2.13 and so I would only place the first target.

I use the candlestick to allocate my risk. Each pattern has its own entry and exit rules, but with the pin bar I assume that if price moves above the high of the active candle (the candle on which the pattern is completed) then my analysis is incorrect and I want to get out of the trade. In the example the high of the pin bar is 1.3497, so my stop loss would be placed at this price.

I then look at the difference between my entry point and my profit target (my reward), and compare it to the difference between my entry point and my stop loss (my risk). If risk is outweighed by reward by a ratio of one-to-two, I will take the trade. For more information about the one-to-two risk-reward ratio I use, see Rule 3 of the 'Risk management' section below.

All of this is illustrated in Figure 2.14, where I have marked on the entry, exit target and stop loss. My entry is at the close of the pin bar, 1.3376; my target at the previous swing low which, in the example, is at 1.2970.

With this entry and these risk parameters my risk and reward can be calculated:

risk = stop loss level - entry level = 1.3497 - 1.3376 = 0.0121 = 121 pips

reward = entry level - profit target level = 1.3376 - 1.2970 = 0.0406 = 406 pips

FIGURE 2.14 – A TYPICAL TRADE

Trade management

The trade management rules of my strategy are very clear. Once entered a trade cannot be altered and must be left alone until either the stop loss or limit order is reached. This is a key aspect of the method, yet it often is the hardest part of the strategy to follow. How to overcome this is examined in more detail in the 'Psychology' section.

Risk management

Risk management is often overlooked by beginners but it is the cornerstone of any successful trading strategy, including mine. I have built solid risk management principles into my strategy and I remain faithful to these principles with every trade I place.

To help you gain a bit more of an understanding of the topic and to illustrate how much of an effect it can have on profitability, I will now outline the three fundamental rules of risk management and illustrate how strict control of risk enables me to tilt the odds in my favour, over the long run, when trading.

Here is a prediction – the majority of readers will get to this section and one of the first things that will spring into their heads will be something like "I already understand risk management, so I can skip this bit." Fine, if you do already understand the concept. If, however, you *think* you understand it, or you feel like you can pick it up as you go along, as I did when I first came across risk management, then I strongly advise you not to skip ahead.

The reason most people feel they can overlook a proper study of risk management is that it seems so obvious: never risk more than you can afford to lose; never risk more than a certain proportion of your account on any one trade; and always keep your losers smaller than your winners. These three rules do pretty much cover everything you need to know but the skill is not in knowing the rules, it is in *following them*. And in order to follow them you must have a genuine understanding of the implications of *not* following them.

One of the biggest barriers to executing risk management correctly is emotion. Psychology plays a massive part in being able to follow your strategy rules and without a strong grasp on what could happen if you don't employ solid risk management it is pretty difficult to recognise the benefits when you do. With this in mind I suggest that even if you already have a strong grasp of how risk management works, a quick scan of the rules I apply to my own strategy can act as a useful refresher.

Rule 1 – Never risk more than you can afford to lose

You should only ever be trading with money that, if lost, would not render you unable to meet your month-to-month financial obligations. What this means is that you should not borrow money from the rainy day pot to fund your account. You should trade a demo account until you have truly disposable funds available.

Many traders read this sort of comment and consider it to be condescending, as if I am suggesting you are unable to manage your household finances. This is very much not the case. The real reason I advise not to risk money you can't afford to lose is because when we trade with money we can't afford to lose, the way we trade with that money changes. Each trade becomes make or break and crushing disappointment follows every loss. When using a strategy that allows for a considerable amount of losing trades, this crushing disappointment can start to influence your trade management and this can render your strategy ineffective.

Consider this: Upon identifying a trade opportunity, you calculate your entry and exit points according to the risk management rules you have set for the pattern involved and they offer a one-to-two risk-reward ratio. Say, for example, a 50 pip risk for a 100 pip gain. On this basis, you enter the trade. It immediately moves in your favour and you soon find yourself 50 pips up on where you bought in. Now, according to strategy rules, we should leave this trade to mature, either into a gain of 100 pips, or a loss of 50.

Theoretically this is easy – just leave it. But say you are trading with the money you would normally put aside for your rent. At 50 pips up, if you book profits you have made a nice gain and you still have your initial rent money, however if the trade were to turn against you, the gain you have seen will be wiped out and the same value deducted from the money you need to meet the rent payment.

Can anybody honestly say that they would be able to remain emotionally objective enough to let the trade mature? I would struggle and I read these rules every night before I sleep.

Rule 2 – Never risk more than a fixed proportion of your account on any one trade

You must set a percentage figure of your account that you will risk on each single trade. If you do not, and if you instead risk a fixed amount in pounds on each trade, you could find that your account is bust after a short succession of losing trades.

For example, if the size of your account is £5000 and you risk £500 on each trade, with ten losing trades in a row you would blow up your account. Ten consecutive losing trades can happen at any time, so you need some method of controlling what you lose that will ensure you live to trade another day.

With a fixed percentage of risk per trade, say 2% of your account, if you do come across a patch of losing trades and your account starts to diminish, the amount you are risking falls in tandem with the size of your account and the risk of losing your entire account is reduced. This is illustrated in Table 2.1.

Of course in the opposite scenario – a succession of winning trades – the amount in pounds you would be risking on each trade would scale up with the total size of your account.

TABLE 2.1 – A SUCCESSION OF LOSING TRADES WITH RISK PER TRADE SET AT 2%

Trade	Account size (£)	Risk per trade (%)	Risk per trade (£)
1	5000	2	100
2	4900	2	98
3	4802	2	96
4	4706	2	94
5	4612	2	92
6	4520	2	90
7	4429	2	89
8	4341	2	87
9	4254	2	85
10	4169	2	83

I do not risk more than 2% to 2.5% of my account on any one trade.

Rule 3 – Aim for a one-to-two risk-reward ratio (keep your winners smaller than your losers)

I am sure you are all familiar with the statistic that a large percentage of foreign exchange traders lose money. The reality is that all traders lose money, but some win more than they lose.

If you have a one-to-two risk-reward ratio this will ensure that you win more on winning trades than you lose on losing trades, and you should stay in business as a trader. When I say that you should use a one-to-two risk-reward ratio I mean that your winning trades should win twice as much as your losing trades lose.

In Table 2.2 I have shown a quick analysis of the outcome of ten trades following this one-to-two risk-to-reward ratio. For the sake of simplicity

I am assuming that a winning trade generates 100 pips profit and a losing trade generates a 50 pip loss.

TABLE 2.2 – RESULTS OF TEN TRADES WITH WINS AND LOSSES

Trade wins	Trade losses	Result
0	10	-500 pips
1	9	-350 pips
2	8	-200 pips
3	7	-50 pips
4	6	+100 pips
5	5	+250 pips
6	4	+400 pips
7	3	+550 pips
8	2	+700 pips
9	1	+850 pips
10	0	+1000 pips

As the table clearly illustrates, even with a win rate of four out of every ten trades, or 40%, by maintaining a one-to-two risk-reward ratio an overall profit will be made. This is good news because no form of analysis, however thorough, produces a win rate of 100%. In fact, very few traders produce a win rate of more than 50%. Maintaining a one-to-two risk-reward ratio also serves to take the pressure out of trading, in that it allows mistakes and losing trades to be made while an overall profit is still possible.

Personally I only insist that I must maintain a positive risk-reward ratio – for me it is not terminal if it is not one-to-two, but I do prefer the ratio to be as close as possible to, or above, one-to-two.

The key thing to take away is that if mistakes are made in our analysis, solid risk management can protect us. Conversely, if mistakes are made in our risk management, no amount of analysis can protect us.

Risk management first, analysis second. Risk management first, analysis second. Risk management first, analysis second, and... Relax.

* * *

That is my trading strategy. As I hope you can see, the trades I make are all based on sound, reasonable logic and are only executed under strict risk management conditions. Controlled application of logic and strict risk management can create long-term profits for a number of strategies – there is not only one strategy that will be successful – but the the approach I have outlined is the one I have found to be effective.

My advice is to trade in a fashion that you are comfortable with. If you like my strategy and feel it is something you could follow then build its features into your own approach. If not, apply your own rules to these concepts and long-term gains can still be achieved.

MY FAVOURITE SETUPS

In this section I describe the three key setups I look for when analysing price action. I consider these to be the reliable, frequent setups that repeatedly offer themselves as an indication of an opportunity. They are:

1. Pin bar
2. Inside day candle
3. Inside day turnaround

The risk management principles I have applied to each setup are the result of my historic analysis of the patterns and their resulting price action.

1. Pin bar

The candlestick pattern I trade most is the pin bar, a bearish version of which is illustrated in Figure 2.15.

FIGURE 2.15 – BEARISH PIN BAR

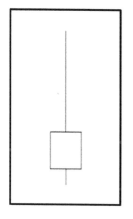

The pin bar is a reversal pattern that often marks the key swings high and low of a trading session, and so can be traded under that assumption.

For a pin bar to form, price is required to close at or near to its opening price, and during the session it is required to have moved considerably in one direction and then to have rebounded. If we break down the pin bar in Figure 2.15 – formed over four hours of trading – into four one-hour candlesticks the price action may look as shown in Figure 2.16.

FIGURE 2.16 – HOURLY REPRESENTATION OF A FOUR-HOUR BEARISH PIN BAR

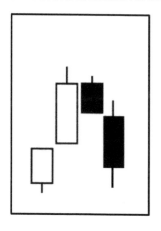

These four hourly candles show that during the first two hours of a four-hour session price rose, then fell during the second two hours. The final hourly candle closes just above the opening price of the first hourly candle.

What a bearish pin bar suggests, for example, is that there is considerable selling pressure above the level at which the bar opened. Enough to return it, once all consolidation has occurred, close to the level at which the session began. This is taken as a sign that there is more selling pressure than buying pressure and so price will likely fall. If this scenario occurs at a level at which price has previously reversed, the likelihood of a second reversal is stronger.

The risk management rules that I apply to the pin bar setup are based upon the assumption that if price breaks the high (or low) of a pin's wick, then my analysis is invalid and I would rather not be in the trade. For this reason, I place my stop loss at the high of a bearish pin bar and the low of a bullish pin bar. The profit target, as previously mentioned, would be placed at the recent swing low if the pin bar is bearish, or at the recent swing high if the pin bar is bullish.

A pin bar having formed, in the majority of cases my entry would be on the opening of the next bar. There are some exceptions. For example, if the pin bar has a particularly long tail, the risk-reward I look for is often not available. This is because the point at which I look to place my profit target – the nearest swing low in a bear market or swing high in a bull market – will be closer to my entry than the extreme of the candlestick's wick (which is where I place my stop). Therefore risk would outweigh reward if I took this trade.

To overcome this I would set an order for entry on a particular retracement of the wick. More often than not this retracement is 50%, meaning that if during the session after the pin bar has formed price moves more than halfway up or down the wick, I will enter. This situation is illustrated in Figure 2.17.

FIGURE 2.17 – ENTRY AT A 50% RETRACEMENT OF A PIN BAR TAIL TO ACHIEVE POSITIVE RISK/REWARD

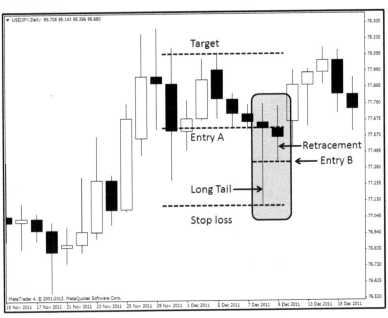

2. Inside day candle

The second most common pattern I trade is the inside day candle. An example is illustrated in Figure 2.18.

FIGURE 2.18 – INSIDE DAY CANDLE

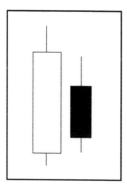

The inside day can be either a reversal or a continuation pattern and so on its own it is neither bullish nor bearish. It often indicates periods of uncertainty in markets and it is the break of either the high or low of the first candle that indicates a directional bias.

For an inside day to form, the price range on a particular day must be completely engulfed by the price range of the previous day. That is, the highs of the day must not exceed the highs of the previous day, and the lows must not exceed the previous day's lows.

I like to consider the inside day as a coiling of a spring that fuels the market. An hourly representation of a daily inside candle would show price moving around considerably during the session, but being unable to break out of the range of the previous day. With price being contained within the channels of the previous session, we assume that once price has found a direction, it will continue to move in such a manner.

More often than not I will trade this pattern as a continuation. This means that if an inside bar formation occurs at key support in an uptrend, I will look to trade to the long side on a break of the *upper limits*. Upper limit can refer to *either* the high of the inside day or the high of the mother day (the day that engulfs the inside day candle). Similarly, if an inside bar formation occurs at key resistance in a downtrend, I will look to trade to the short side on a break of the lower limits of the inside day or mother day candle.

The more risk averse and reliable method is to wait for a break of the mother day, but sometimes, because of the size of the mother candle, this offers steep risk-reward and so is untradeable. If this is the case, and I feel strongly that the setup meets all the other conditions of my trade strategy, I will sometimes trade a break of the inside day. Whilst inherently more risky, as the weaker setup is less likely to play out, it enables me to reduce my risk and increase the potential profit I can take.

The profit target for this setup is placed at a historic level of support or resistance, such as a swing low or a swing high. In terms of risk management, I place my stop at the low (or high) of the mother session: low if the pattern is a bullish one, high if bearish. If price reaches and falls beyond these levels, my analysis is invalid and I no longer want to be in the trade.

3. Inside day turnaround

The inside day turnaround, as indicated by its name, is an alternative way to play the inside bar strategy. Key to the inside bar turnaround is the direction of the trend the pattern occurs within. The active candle is the session after the inside candle and it must break the mother bar *against* the trend and then return to a price within the mother bar's range. An example of a bearish inside day turnaround pattern is illustrated in Figure 2.19.

FIGURE 2.19 - BEARISH INSIDE DAY TURNAROUND

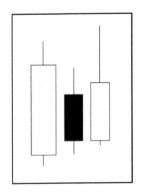

This is a continuation pattern that indicates pressure on one side of a market; often pressure enough to cause a considerable movement in prices.

A look at the hourly representation of this pattern would show price primarily being contained within the highs and lows of the mother session, until, against the trend, one of these levels is breached. Within the daily session, however, price returns to within the parameters of the mother bar.

My directional bias is formed based on the breach. If price breaks the upper limit of the mother bar, then returns, it suggests that selling pressure is strong and my directional bias is to the short side. Conversely, if price breaks the lower limit of the mother bar, then returns, it suggests that buying pressure is strong and my directional bias is to the long side.

I like to trade this pattern at the close of the active candle. This means that in the case of a bullish inside bar turnaround pattern, once the breakaway session – the third candle in the pattern – is closed, I enter the trade.

My profit target is again placed at a previous support or resistance level. The risk management principles I apply to this pattern are similar to that of the standard inside bar, with the highs (or lows) of the mother bar acting as stop loss positions.

* * *

The three patterns I have described are the major signals I will look for on any trading day. Whilst there are more patterns available, I feel these three are the most reliable in terms of producing the expected results. They occur frequently enough on the daily charts across a selection of the major currency pairs that I do not need to trade the less reliable patterns.

Sometimes if a pattern I consider to be more risky falls in line with the parameters of my strategy I will consider it, as you will see in my trading diary. In those cases, I will address the mechanics of those particular patterns when they arise.

MARKET EXAMPLES

I will now present a few examples of trades that offer differing risk-reward ratios. As I have mentioned, the risk-reward available on each trade is effectively the green and red light of trading. Having identified an opportunity, it is important to consider whether this opportunity falls in line with your risk-reward rules. If it does, green light. If not, red light, and you wait until a trade comes along that does fit the rules.

It is relatively simple to calculate the levels of risk and reward that a trade offers and the more you trade the quicker you will be able to tell if a setup presents an opportunity or whether it is in your best interests to sit it out.

A positive risk-reward setup

The chart in Figure 2.20 shows a bearish pin bar forming close to a level that has acted as support in the past, and which as a result may act as resistance in the near future. The assumption is that the down trend is likely to continue and so I look for a selling opportunity as soon as the pin bar is complete.

FIGURE 2.20 – BEARISH PIN ENTRY OFFERING POSITIVE RISK-REWARD

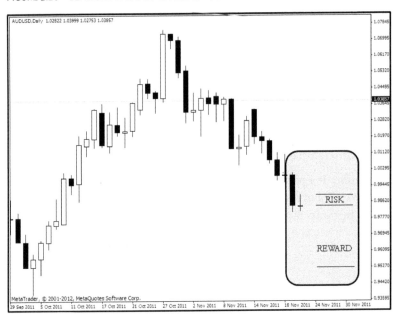

Would I enter this trade?

First I must consider where price is trading now and where it is likely to go if my analysis is correct. The current market price is 0.9833. Based on the rules set out by the strategy in relation to this pattern, I look for price to reach its previous swing low and this becomes my primary target. Looking at Figure 2.17 the previous swing low was on 4 October, at 0.9526. The gap between current price (0.9833) and target price (0.9526) becomes reward (*R*).

With pin bars, my strategy dictates that the point at which my analysis becomes invalid is at the tail end of the pin bar – in this instance the high of the pin's wick, at 0.9898. The gap between current price (0.9833) and my stop loss (0.9898) becomes risk (r).

For the trade to be worthwhile, it must offer a one-to-two risk-to-reward ratio, meaning R must be twice the size of r. In the example shown entry is at 0.9833, profit target is at 0.9526 and stop loss is at 0.9898.

Therefore:

r = 0.9898 - 0.9833 = 0.0065, or 65 pips

R = 0.9833 - 0.9526 = 0.0307, or 307 pips

R is more than twice as big as r so I would enter the trade.

Let's look at what happened to the trade setup. The development of price action for this trade is shown in Figure 2.21. As you can see, my trade would have been stopped out for a loss of 65 pips on 12 October.

FIGURE 2.21 – STOPPED OUT AT PIN BAR HIGH ON 12 OCTOBER

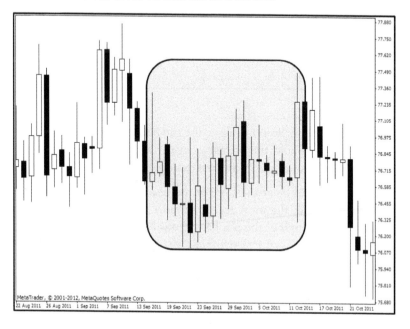

A negative risk-reward setup

Figure 2.22 shows a similar situation, however this market has seen a much shallower decline. Conceptually I would approach this opportunity in the same way as the first, so would I have entered a trade?

FIGURE 2.22 – BEARISH PIN ENTRY OFFERING NEGATIVE RISK-REWARD

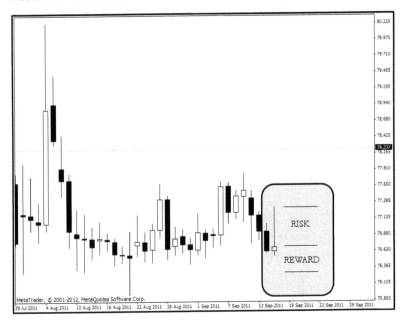

As a result of the shallower decline, the gap between the current price – my entry point – and the primary target I set at previous support is much smaller than it was in the first example.

Here, entry would be at the close of the bearish pin, 76.68; the profit target would be at the most recent support, 76.31; and the stop loss would be at the high of the pin bar, 77.24. Note that support is taken from a level *at which price reversed more than once*, not the low of the 19 August wick, which would be at 75.95.

The calculations give $r = 0.56$, or 56 pips, and $R = 0.37$, or 37 pips. In this example R is not twice as large as r. I cannot achieve a one-to-two risk-reward ratio and so I would not enter the trade.

PSYCHOLOGY

The final piece of my foreign exchange trading approach is another that is often overlooked by traders, but its application is vital to my success. I will start by saying that I am no psychologist. The areas I cover here are strictly with reference to trading and the mental attitude I take towards my trading.

Faith

The first key aspect of the psychology of foreign exchange trading is *faith*.

To have faith in your strategy suggests you are confident that the trades you identify, executed in accordance with the risk management rules you apply to them, will result in long-term gains. If you do not have this belief and you are unable to trust in long-term results, you will find it very hard to take losses.

If you find it hard to take losses, when a string of them comes along it is very easy to blame a particular aspect of your strategy and alter that aspect. This alteration could replace the string of winners you were due under your old strategy rules with a string of losers associated with the new strategy.

As you can probably see, this could result in a downward spiral of losing trades. There is no point in following a strategy if you do not have faith that its rules will produce a favourable outcome in the long term.

Control

The second key aspect of trading psychology is *control*.

Control refers to having the emotional strength to implement each aspect of your strategy objectively, and to stick to and manage your trades accordingly. Control is born out of having faith in your methods.

In our execution of trades, we must be completely emotionally detached from the amount we are risking. This sounds ridiculous, but if we consider that we have strict risk management rules in place that ensure that we will not go bust, and that we do not risk too much on each trade, then why shouldn't we be emotionally detached? Any level of attachment towards profits or losses before the targets are hit could result in an early exit from a trade, which will act to invalidate the rules we have put in place to protect us.

Patience

The third key aspect of trading psychology is *patience.*

Consider how many times you have identified a possible trade opportunity, not been 100% happy with it, but taken it anyway. Regardless of whether this trade is a winner or a loser, we must ask ourselves why we took it. As traders, naturally we want to execute trades. That is what we do. What we must not do, however, is execute trades for this reason alone. I have fallen foul of this in the past and each time I had the same result.

To illustrate – having identified a possible opportunity, I have applied my strategy rules to a price scenario. The trade looks pretty good, but say for example that a pin bar has formed some way short of a key level. I could take the trade now, as it looks like it could be due for a reversal, but without the key level the likelihood is reduced and my risk analysis is less accurate.

Alternatively, I could wait until another trade comes along with a higher likelihood of playing out, that does meet all the requirements of my strategy. I am feeling a little impatient this day and so I take the trade. Invariably, it goes against me and a better setup presents itself a few days later. If I had been patient and trusted my strategy to present enough opportunities then I wouldn't have taken a loss and could have entered the new, stronger setup. As is now the case, I am entering the setup with a loss on the same pair a few days earlier, which I must make up to profit on aggregate.

* * *

With each trade you take, the key aspects of the psychology required will become clearer in their application and easier to follow. It is important to realise that as humans we are emotional beings and that nothing affects our emotions more than money, so in the beginning it is natural for the mindset required to feel uncomfortable. Over time this will fade and so long as your psychological approach to the trades you make matures alongside your strategy, you will get there.

As a target, psychologically, a trader should reach the point where the emotions they take from their trading day are not governed by how many trades they won or lost, or even by how much they made in the market, but by how closely they adhered to their strategy.

You must learn to be content with a losing day if throughout that day the trades you made were in strict accordance with the rules you follow, and vice versa, you must not be content with a winning day if you have generated the profits by breaking your own rules. It may have paid off today, but in the long run it will not.

Chapter Three

My Trading Diary

Having outlined the way I trade, I am now ready to start my live trading diary. I have been trading the strategy I will use in the diary for a number of years and over these years I have seen reliable long-term gains. In this diary I will record three months of trading from January 2012 through to March 2012.

For reference purposes, I have included in the Appendix the 2011 charts for the three major pairs I trade throughout.

These gains are of course intertwined with periods of draw down and so it impossible to state with any certainty whether or not my strategy, applied over the period in question, will produce a net profit or a net loss. What I can assure you is that I will present complete transparency for the trades I take, sound reasoning in their execution and a logical explanation of my thought processes throughout the period.

Although I do not like to get hung up on losing trades, I will often investigate the reasons why they did not go as I expected – not to alter anything on that particular trade, but to detect any recurring problems with my strategy. I will include this analysis alongside each trade.

In terms of presentation, for each trade I will outline the pattern I am looking at and the levels at which I am looking for it to form, as well as the risk management parameters I am applying and the justification of this analysis, for example why I have chosen a particular target, etc.

At the end of each month traded, I will collate and present the results, which will be analysed and evaluated in the final section of the book.

Throughout the diary, I will include a narrative of anything that I feel might explain my actions in more detail, or of anything that I feel might (or might not) be useful to your own trading.

MONTH 1

Sunday, 1 January 2012

So here goes. Welcome to my trading diary.

It being Sunday, the market is of course closed, with the business week ahead running from 2 January to 6 January.

I start the month in something of a sombre mood as my strategy has been somewhat pummelled over the last month or so, with many of my trades going against my judgment. Historically throughout December trading activity is relatively muted and otherwise effective strategies can be rendered useless against the backdrop of a weak market. With this in mind I have convinced myself that I am not to feel too downtrodden, but leading up to the writing of the diary I had been hoping for a smooth run and unfortunately for me it has been a white river of a month.

On the bright side, what it does enable me to do is demonstrate the first aspect of trading psychology outlined in this book; faith in my methods. I have been trading this same strategy, plus or minus a few tweaks, for around four years. Each year I have consistently profited from the market and the majority of my losses have come from *off* months, during which for whatever reason conditions have not played out in my favour.

Soon enough these conditions have always fallen back in line with the profitable side of my plan. So long as I can keep this in mind, I can approach January with the mindset that I am due a string of winners, but only if I trade my rules properly.

At the beginning of each month I like to take stock of what happened in the previous month in each of the three major pairs I trade – EUR/USD, AUD/USD and USD/JPY – and in turn what I might expect from the coming month. This can include expected price action, but also any historical patterns that I feel are worth mentioning, as well as any upcoming important events that may affect markets.

EUR/USD

What happened in December?

In EUR/USD there was a period of relative indecision during the first week or so of December 2011, with price contained within November's high and low. Towards the end of the second week, there was a considerable and sharp decline, with price falling below key support around 1.3170.

Price then climbed back up to this level, only to be rejected, with former support turning into resistance. Notably this rejection is illustrated by the pin bar at 21 December (see Figure 3.1).

FIGURE 3.1 - EUR/USD IN DECEMBER 2011

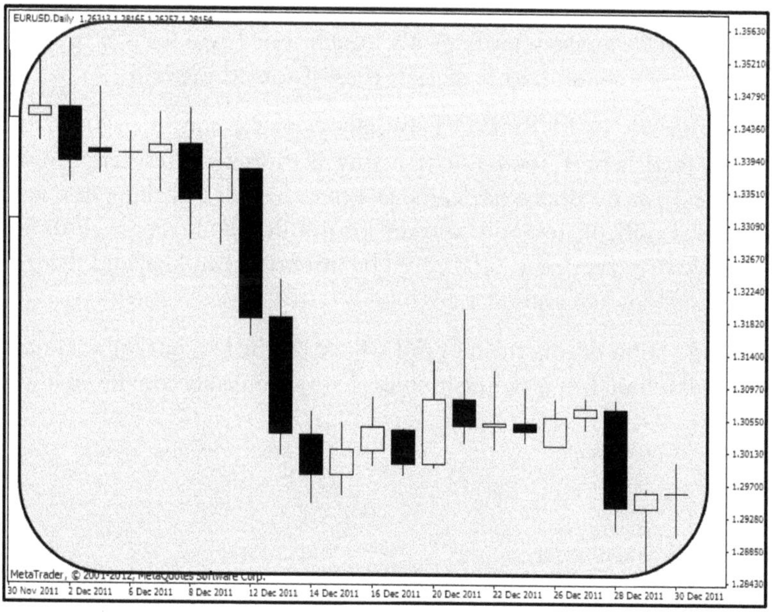

What might happen in January?

Having broken a key support level, price seems to have met interim support at around 1.3030. This has been tested in the later days of December and a pin bar has formed around the 1.3000 level suggesting a certain amount of buying pressure exists below it. Taking this pin bar into consideration, there may be a kick in prices towards 1.3030, which could become resistance before the downtrend continues.

One of the most well-known market phenomena occurs this month – the January Effect. The January Effect is the tendency for markets to post either lows or highs during the month that will remain in effect until at least the middle of the year, if not for its entirety.

Applying this to the month just gone and the month that lies ahead, we could be heading for a reversal to the upside. I make this assumption based on the fact that EUR/USD has been down trending for the majority of the previous year and the January Effect has shown reversal points in the past.

Of course when it comes to picking tops or bottoms great care is needed. I will not be actively trading this hunch, but I will keep it in mind should price action start to suggest there is something in it.

In summary, in EUR/USD I initially expect a continuation of the downtrend, with 1.3000-1.3030 acting as short-term resistance to the upside. In terms of downside, the fact that the pair is making new lows makes it difficult to apply a lower limit, but a look way back to last January suggests that 1.2900 could be important, and beyond that the mid-2010 lows of around 1.2650.

At some point during the month I will be on the lookout for a reversal, but will refrain from trading it unless I am completely convinced it will occur.

AUD/USD

What happened in December?

In AUD/USD price tumbled to its monthly low for the first couple of weeks. Support was found around the 0.9900 level. From this support a sizable surge was mounted, returning price almost to the point from which it fell. This is illustrated in Figure 3.2.

FIGURE 3.2 – AUD/USD IN DECEMBER 2011

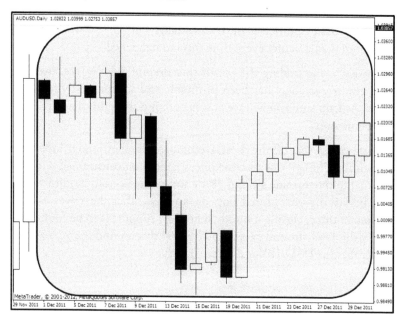

What might happen in January?

I will look for the buying strength seen in December to continue, especially if price can break through and close above the 1.0200 support area. If this is occurs, I expect price to head initially towards the 1.0380 resistance area and perhaps on towards 1.0500.

In summary, I will look for opportunities to buy into the pair, with this bias being reinforced by a close above immediately apparent resistance.

USD/JPY

What happened in December?

Since this is the first day of the first month of this diary, I feel now is as good a time as any to describe my relationship with USD/JPY. I hate it as a currency pair. It seems to take pleasure in proving my analysis wrong or, even if I am right, it seems to know to the pip where I have placed my stop loss.

If I had a penny for every time a USD/JPY trade has gone against me, hit my stop, then reversed and moved in the direction I expected all along, I would be a rich man. Unfortunately, in the real world, I have lost more than a penny every time this has happened.

What keeps me trading the pair is that despite these gripes, over the long run my strategy has been profitable and so financially it makes sense. As I am sure you will see at some point during this diary, the pair drives me nuts.

Having gotten that off my chest, December was an extremely indecisive month for USD/JPY, with close prices remaining constrained within a channel to the top side around 78.15 and to the bottom around 77.55. Just before the year closed out, on 30 December there was a steep decline in price, closing around 76.86. Key support is to be found just below this level, around 76.50, and beyond that around the 76.10 level. December for USD/JPY is illustrated in Figure 3.3.

FIGURE 3.3 - USD/JPY IN DECEMBER 2011

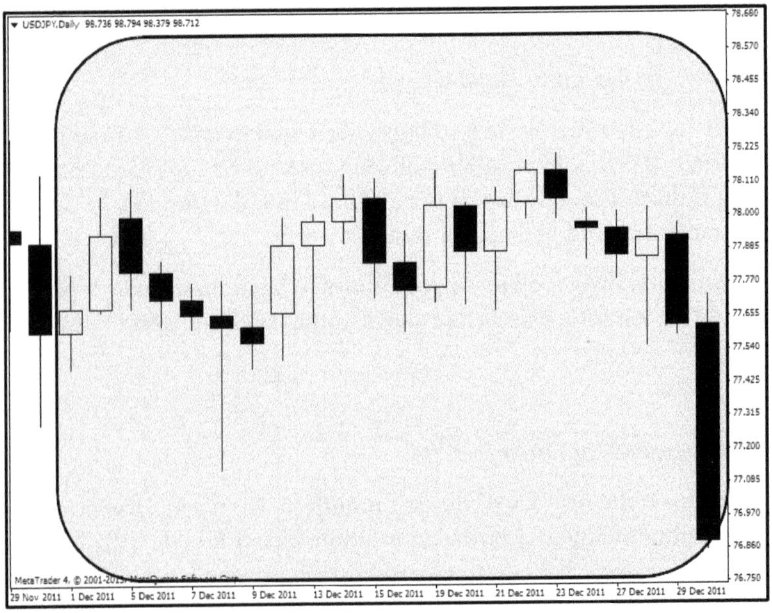

What might happen in January?

With no real direction being determined in December it is hard to know exactly what the pair will do in the weeks to come. By nature of its composition, USD/JPY is pitting two of the strongest currencies against each other, which can often cause prolonged range-bound action until a key fundamental factor allows a trend to be established. With this in mind I would suggest that the recent end-of-December low could see its progress halted and price could return to test the support from which it fell, around 77.50-60.

In summary, last month's indecision and the sharp drop towards the end of the month suggests I should stay out of this pair until a clear directional trend presents itself. Having said this, with price having fallen towards a key support level, if any candlestick patterns do arise it may be worth considering a range trade looking back up towards the 77.50-60 area.

Monday, 2 January 2012 – 10pm GMT

First trading day complete! Notoriously a quiet one, the first day back after the holidays has lived up to its lacklustre reputation. With most trading activity not resumed until tomorrow, a quick glance across the major pairs doesn't inspire much. There are, however, a couple of things I would like to show you.

1. Pin bar in USD/JPY

The first of these is the pin bar that has formed in USD/JPY. Illustrated in Figure 3.4, a first look suggests that this could be an opportunity, but there are some things I must consider before jumping into the trade.

FIGURE 3.4 – PIN BAR FORMATION IN USD/JPY

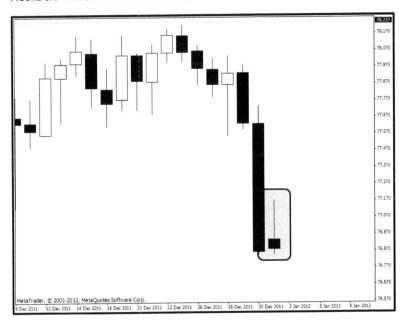

First of all, I have to take into account that at the end of December the pair dropped considerably, towards the lower end of its range. At this point, two things can happen. The pair could reverse, holding its range, and trade sideways for a while then upwards. Alternatively the pair could break through the support it is heading towards and a downtrend could be initiated. If I was to trade this bearish pin bar I would have to be sure that this range was not going to hold, or at least have some indication that this is the case. At present I have no such indication.

Second, I have to consider my risk management parameters. The entry point would be at the close that has just been posted at 76.88. A look at the key historic price levels tells me that the next key support comes in at around 76.57 (the low of 18/11/12), which if used as a primary target will offer 31 pips reward. My stop would be placed just above the high of the active candle, around 77.01, which works out as about 13 pips risk. This gives me a risk-reward ratio of slightly better than one-to-two, which is OK.

What will I do?

You might be surprised to read that I have decided to turn the trade down. To trade a pattern that has been formed on such a weak trading day is dangerous and with the hammering I have taken in this pair as of late I really am looking for a much stronger trade to start the year. It is worth noting that a more aggressive trader may take this on for a small gain of 25-30 pips and they would be perfectly justified in doing so, but this is not one for me. We will see if I have missed out in the days to come.

2. AUD/USD closes above 1.0170

The second thing I would like to show you is not a pattern as such, but a bit of analysis nonetheless. Having struggled to close above 1.0170 for the past couple of weeks, AUD/USD finally did so on the last day of December.

This close has been emulated today, with another strong close above what could now act as support. If 1.0170 does turn out to be a new support level, I expect a small rise over the coming days in this pair, then a retest of this level. It is the retest that I will look to trade, if a pattern emerges. This situation is illustrated in Figure 3.5.

FIGURE 3.5 – DECISIVE DAILY CLOSE IN AUD/USD

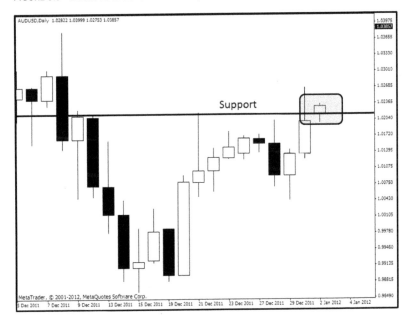

Wednesday, 4 January 2012

I have spotted what looks to be a nice opportunity for a trade in AUD/USD. This is shown in Figure 3.6.

FIGURE 3.6 – PIN BAR FORMATION IN AUD/USD

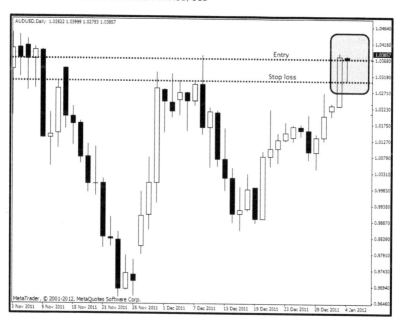

Having closed above a previous resistance level, the pair saw a solid rise yesterday, closing just shy of what now becomes key resistance at about 1.0390. Today price fell, reclaiming around half of yesterday's gains, but then quickly rose, forming a bullish candle in the process.

Risk-reward looks good, with the low at 1.0303 offering a risk of about 58-60 pips if I buy in now, and a possible target, based on previous key levels, all the way up at 1.0750, offering reward of about 380 pips.

Every so often an opportunity comes along that presents an extremely attractive risk-reward ratio and this seems to be one of them. One thing I should be wary of is that resistance at 1.0390 could hold as an upper range, which could send price back down to previous support. My risk management will ensure that if this is the case, my loss will not be too damaging.

Trade 1

Pair	AUD/USD
Order	1.0361 BUY
Stop loss	1.0303
Limit	1.0750
Risk	58
Reward	389

There are no other real opportunities elsewhere, so I will get some sleep and check the pairs again tomorrow.

One of the most desirable aspects of the strategy I trade is its *set and forget* nature. Once I have entered a trade, my risk management conditions take care of the mechanical side of things, so all I have to do is wait for the outcome. The fact that most of my trades are made at New York close means I can make my trades, apply the relevant risk management parameters and let them mature overnight.

Thursday, 5 January 2012

Disaster! One look at the price action in today's AUD/USD shows the trade I made yesterday (Trade 1) was premature. A surge in the USD across the board means I have been stopped out for a loss at my predefined stop loss level of 1.0303, as shown in Figure 3.7.

FIGURE 3.7 – STOPPED OUT OF AUD/USD

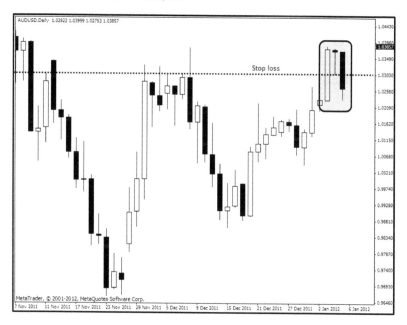

It looks as though some good data has come out of the US, with new jobless claims falling by more than expected, which could explain the action. My first trade of the year results in a 58 pip loss. NEXT!

Monday, 9 January 2012

Take a look at the daily chart for AUD/USD shown in Figure 3.8. Still reeling from my first loss of the year, an opportunity has arisen for a similar trade at a better price.

FIGURE 3.8 – RE-ENTRY OPPORTUNITY THROUGH PIN BAR IN AUD/USD

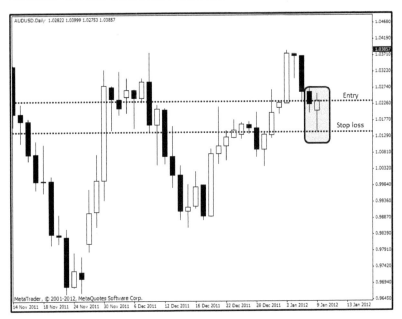

Having fallen considerably over the past couple of days, price was nearing its range support at around 1.0170. Throughout today price has dropped to that level, then quickly returned to form a pin bar, right on support.

A look at the risk options available tells me that stop placement would be at 1.0144, the pin bar's low, with primary target at previous resistance at 1.0380. If price can break through this resistance, there could be a more substantial move up towards the level I targeted with my previous trade in this pair, but until I see a price pattern to confirm this, the more conservative target is my best bet.

Trade 2

Pair	AUD/USD
Order	1.0237 BUY
Stop loss	1.0144
Limit	1.0380
Risk	93
Reward	143

Very little else has presented itself as worth mentioning over the course of the past few days, even less has presented itself as worth trading.

I can start to feel the frustration of a slow month creeping in, something I must get under control as soon as possible. This sort of frustration has led to me making silly trades in the past and I am determined not to allow this to happen. I am consciously avoiding the more exotic pairings, as I am sure something would tempt me, perhaps against my better judgment. Trades should not be born of impatience.

Tuesday, 10 January 2012

Figure 3.9 shows the daily chart for EUR/USD.

FIGURE 3.9 – BEARISH PIN FORMATION IN EUR/USD

EUR/USD saw a steep decline towards the end of last week, with the first couple of days this week forming a correction of about 40% to 50% against the decline. Today's price action has formed a bearish pin bar, which presents an opportunity for a sell trade. Although the trade looks good the pattern has formed shy of a key level, so before the decline continues there could be more upside to go.

Sometimes when an opportunity such as this presents itself I like to tighten my risk parameters to reflect my uncertainty. Normally this entails setting 2x risk as my target, regardless of key levels. When targets are set in this way, a quick pop in price movement can be all it takes for a target to be hit.

The trade is as follows: I will trade the pin bar, with risk set as the difference between the bar's close price at 1.2776 and its upper limit at 1.2817. Risk is thus 41 pips. Looking for reward to be around 2x risk, I will set it at 1.2692, which will be 84 pips.

With the pair having encountered selling pressure above its current price, I feel I am justified in trading a further decline in the pair. My conservative target of 1.2692 is based upon 2x risk, but also falls nicely around the swing low that preceded the correction.

Trade 3

Pair	EUR/USD
Order	1.2776 SELL
Stop loss	1.2817
Limit	1.2692
Risk	41
Reward	84

Wednesday, 11 January 2012

Target hit (Trade 3, 10 January)! Today's action in EUR/USD saw a dollar gain, driving the price of the pair downwards. Price quickly fell to the support posted on 9 January, hitting my target of 1.2692 in the process. See Figure 3.10. The result is an 84 pip profit on my trade.

FIGURE 3.10 – PROFIT TARGET HIT IN EUR/USD

Taking a quick look at the other pairs I can see that AUD/USD also posted a bullish pin bar today, midway between the support and resistance channels I identified at the beginning of the week. This is shown in Figure 3.11.

No trade is available, as my strategy stipulates this formation must be at or near a key level, but I am still long in this pair as of my trade on 9 January, so although there is no apparent opportunity, the new pin bar candle is a reinforcement of my earlier judgment.

FIGURE 3.11 – PIN BAR FORMATION IN AUD/USD

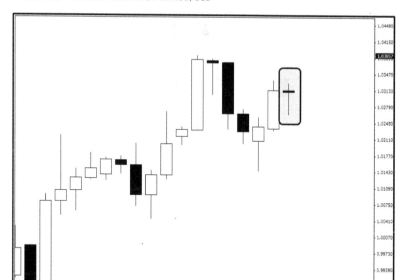

MetaTrader, © 2001-2012, MetaQuotes Software Corp.

USD/JPY also posted a similar pin today, suggesting downward pressure in the pair. You can see this in Figure 3.12. In a similar vein to the candle posted back at the beginning of the month, a lack of any direction in the pair (other than sideways) makes me reluctant to place a trade.

FIGURE 3.12 – PIN BAR FORMATION IN USD/JPY

Although the pin has formed at support, the fact that it sits just above does not really give me any clue as to how price might act if it fell below this price. A trade could really only be justified if the pin was to close below support, as this would suggest that not only is there selling pressure at the higher prices, but also that selling pressure is enough to force a close below a previous key level. At this point I am not convinced this is the case. This is one for me to keep an eye on.

Monday, 16 January 2012

An interesting development presented itself in EUR/USD today. This pair that I have recently been bearish on, as per my trade on 10 January, has posted a couple of really violent days. Price fell to my target – as already mentioned – then turned quickly at support, shooting up to resistance in a day, then falling from resistance back down to support yesterday. A look at the chart in Figure 3.13 shows price breaking support yesterday at about 1.2661, but closing above it.

FIGURE 3.13 – BULLISH PIN BAR FORMATION IN EUR/USD

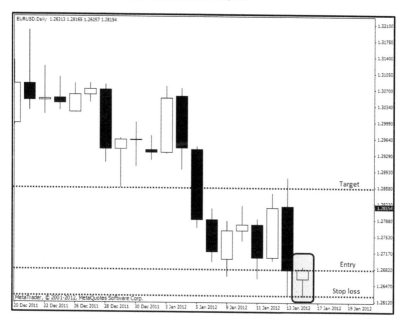

Today's action has formed a bullish pin bar at this level, with the candle's suggested bias being reinforced by the fact that the pair broke below the 1.2661 level one more time, but once again was unable to close below it.

A long trade in this pair offers a good risk-reward ratio, with a stop placed at the low of the candle, 1.2625, and a target of 1.2857 as posted by the previous swing low on 29 December.

There is an air of caution about the trade, as a look at historical action tells me that the past couple of days have seen new lows on the pair dating way back to August 2010, but the signal is a solid one. Who knows, this could be the January Effect taking hold, in which case we could see a substantial kick higher. This is one of my riskier trades.

Trade 4

Pair	EUR/USD
Order	1.2665 BUY
Stop loss	1.2625
Limit	1.2857
Risk	40
Reward	192

Tuesday, 17 January 2012

Target hit (Trade 2, 9 January)! Having missed my target by 3 pips on 12 January, my long AUD/USD trade placed back on 9 January has reached its target today. What turned out to be a nice inside (Friday/Monday) pin bar yesterday seems to have propelled prices upwards, breaking the monthly range resistance, hitting my target and then closing back below it. This action is shown in Figure 3.14. My gain is 143 pips.

FIGURE 3.14 - PROFIT TARGET HIT IN AUD/USD

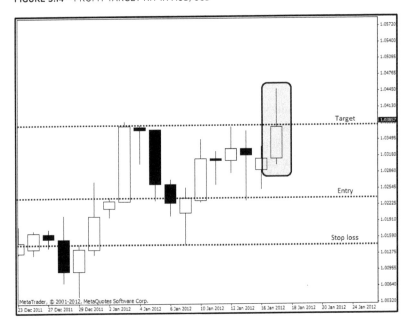

Two things are now likely to happen in AUD/USD. If price fails to close above resistance for a second day, then I expect the range to be held and prices to fall towards the support from which I placed the trade.

Conversely, if I see a solid break of resistance with a close above it, this pair could move up towards the highs posted last October, around 1.0750. I will look to the price candles to hint at which of these scenarios is more likely throughout the rest of the week.

In addition to this, I am looking at USD/JPY today. Having been reluctant to place a trade in USD/JPY so far this month due to the uncertainty reflected in the price action, and now with my confidence buoyed by a nice take in the Aussie, I have finally been tempted into playing my hand.

Price action today has formed a strong bullish candle, breaking below support at around 76.67 and returning to close above it, as shown in Figure 3.15.

FIGURE 3.15 – PIN BAR FORMATION IN USD/JPY

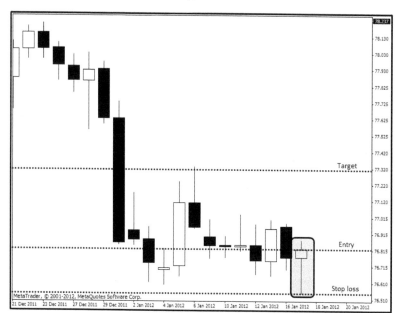

This candle at support offers a pretty tight stop at the bar's low of 76.54, with a target of around 77.30, as per the monthly highs.

Trade 5

Pair	USD/JPY
Order	76.81 BUY
Stop loss	76.54
Limit	77.30
Risk	27
Reward	49

Wednesday, 18 January 2012

Today's action in the US dollar shows just how fickle the currency markets can be in response to economic data. Although it was positive overall, industrial production data came in at slightly lower than expected and this caused some really choppy action in the lower time frames in the major USD pairs. Fortunately, my strategy enables me to sidestep the choppy action and perform my analysis once the market has posted its daily close.

Looking at the charts reveals two developments worthy of note.

The first is a target hit, in my EUR/USD trade from 16 January (Trade 4). Price rose substantially pretty much all day and broke my target of 1.2857 before turning at 1.2867 and closing at 1.2862. This is illustrated in Figure 3.16. My gain is 232 pips.

FIGURE 3.16 – PROFIT TARGET HIT IN EUR/USD

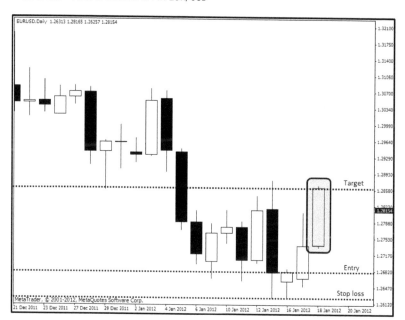

The second is an inside day that has formed in the Aussie dollar, as shown in Figure 3.17.

FIGURE 3.17 – INSIDE DAY FORMATION IN AUD/USD

Although the pattern requires a break of the mother bar to become tradeable, I can form a bias based around the key levels. As alluded to a few days ago, a close above the monthly range resistance could indicate the beginnings of an uptrend in this market.

It could be argued that the pair has been trending steadily upwards since November last year and so if this pattern completes and signals an opportunity I will look to buy the pair upwards towards the aforementioned October highs around 1.0750. It is these low-risk, high-reward opportunities that if taken advantage of can really swing a trading year's bottom line, so this is very much one to watch towards the end of the week.

Thursday, 19 January 2012

Yet another bias-reinforcing candle has formed in AUD/USD. Looking at the chart I showed yesterday, but with today's action included, there is a bullish pin bar forming at what now seems to have become support in a possible uptrend continuation in this pair. See Figure 3.18.

FIGURE 3.18 – BULLISH PIN BAR FORMATION IN AUD/USD

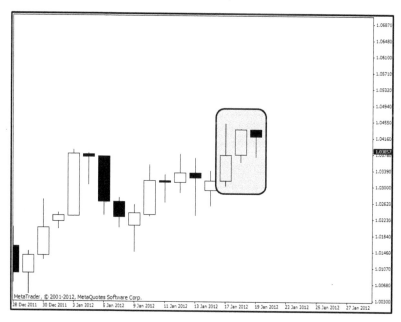

Whilst still strictly not tradeable according to my strategy rules, this is a strong sign that the bias I formed yesterday could see itself vindicated before long. Whilst it is tempting to trade the pin, I have seen these reverse in the past and as the pattern was initially recognised as an inside day this is how I must trade it. With this in mind I will watch closely for a break of the mother bar's high at 1.0449.

Whilst not tradeable in itself, the pin bar offers me a useful risk indication, with its low presenting itself as the immediate candidate for stop placement. I have placed an entry order based upon a mother bar break, which if triggered to create a trade I will log in the diary on its trigger day.

One thing to be wary of is the fact that the pair has risen pretty much all week and historically Friday is the day that some of these gains are given back, but at the risk of over-analysis I will leave it there and see what tomorrow brings.

Also of note today is a target hit on my USD/JPY trade of a few days ago (Trade 5, 17 January). This is shown in Figure 3.19. My gain is 49 pips.

FIGURE 3.19 – PROFIT TARGET HIT IN USD/JPY

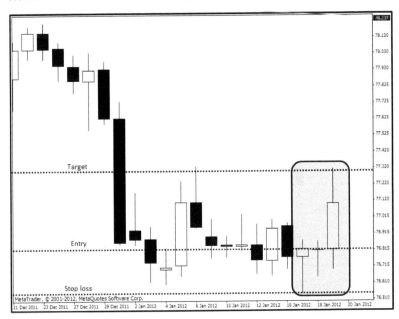

This trade gives a nice illustration of how careful target placement can be the difference between booking profits and letting those profits turn into a loss. If you recall my target was placed at 77.30, the monthly high, which also happened to be the previous month's swing low. This confluence of swing points is no coincidence and with relatively little difficulty it was identifiable as a key point.

Price today has seen the pair hit this level almost to the pip, before correcting downwards. If I had been greedy in my placement, this target could have been missed and I may well have seen price fall tomorrow back to its support, wiping out any would-be profits.

The lesson here is that I always need to have a reason for target placement. I do not set a target because it is where I *want* price to go.

Friday, 20 January 2012

Here we go! The entry point in AUD/USD I set yesterday was hit during today's trading in the Aussie. My entry was triggered at 1.0450 (a break of the mother candle formed on 17 January) with my stop placed at the low of yesterday's pin, at 1.0370.

If I was slightly more risk tolerant, I could have placed my stop at the low of the mother bar as this would still have been within my risk-reward parameters, but the confluence of a pin bar and the key support level gives me confidence that the price to watch is yesterday's low.

Any fall below this would negate the bias and suggest a continuation of range-bound pricing, in which case I would not want to be in the trade. A look back over the last six months of trading gives me a clear target of around 1.0750, the October highs of last year.

Trade 6

Pair	AUD/USD
Order	1.0450 BUY
Stop loss	1.0370
Limit	1.0750
Risk	80
Reward	300

Another point of note in today's action was an inside candle formed in USD/JPY. Having reached range-bound support, price went back mid-range today, but remained well within the constraints of the previous day. This is shown in Figure 3.20.

FIGURE 3.20 – INSIDE BAR FORMATION IN USD/JPY

A quick glance at the candlestick formed suggests the bias may well be to the downside, as a bearish pin bar has developed, but this is not confirmed until the mother candle is broken, so no trade should be placed yet.

If the mother candle is broken to the downside and if price can remain below range support, this could be the beginning of a larger downward move. Alternatively, if the bar is broken to the upside, price could move up towards 78.00 without seeing much key level resistance. This is one to keep an eye on.

Monday, 23 January 2012

Today there is very little to remark upon, but in the spirit of full disclosure I need to note that I have placed an entry order on either side of the USD/JPY inside candle I mentioned on Friday. If this entry is triggered I will note the full trade details as usual, but for now it is enough to say that my orders sit at either end of the mother candle, a buy just above the high and a sell just below the low.

This is what's commonly known as a saddle trade. It is a method I normally try to avoid as I really like to form a strong directional bias before entering a trade. In this pair though it is hard to form a bias due to its inherent nature. The Japanese yen and the US dollar are both seen as safe haven currencies (the dollar historically, the yen more recently so). This means they often strengthen or weaken in tandem with each other, depending on risk trends.

This in-tandem movement often makes for indecisive price action (as has been the case throughout January), but it can also lead to some substantial moves in short periods of time. I think of this pair as two tectonic plates moving together. Every so often one gains a little bit of momentum of the other and what was a slow moving equilibrium becomes very one sided. Big price jumps or falls are like sudden earthquakes.

It is very hard to tell whether price will rise or fall, and as with an earthquake it can be even harder to say when. In this sort of situation a saddle trade guarantees entry at the price you have identified as a signal point, whichever direction price goes in.

Tuesday, 24 January 2012

Vindicated! My saddle trade has been placed with my entry order being hit today. Whilst my initial bias was to the downside, the way I arranged my entry options took into account that price may well move upwards and if it did I would want to be in the trade. This is exactly what happened, as you can see in Figure 3.21.

FIGURE 3.21 - INSIDE BAR ENTRY IN USD/JPY

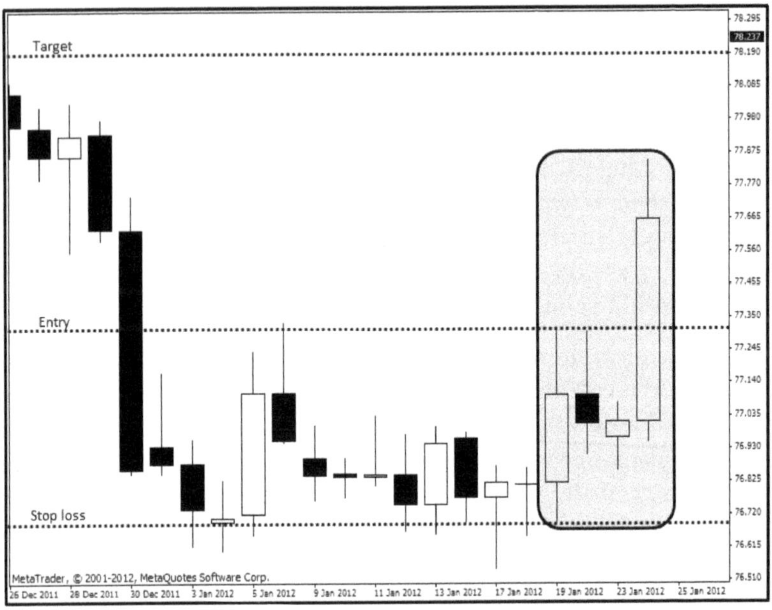

My order was filled at 77.31, with my target placed at 78.19. In terms of risk management, this would be considered one of my more risky trades of the month with my stop at the low of the mother bar all the way down at 76.69. However, I feel my target is well placed in the resistance region seen throughout December just above the 78.00 flat level and this is enough to warrant the risk.

Trade 7

Pair	USD/JPY
Order	77.31 BUY
Stop loss	76.69
Limit	78.19
Risk	62
Reward	88

A further opportunity to trade has presented itself in EUR/USD, as shown in Figure 3.22.

FIGURE 3.22 – BULLISH PIN BAR FORMATION IN EUR/USD

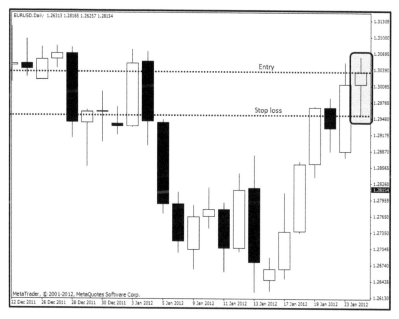

A look at the chart shows a bullish pin bar forming, with price dropping to support, reversing and then climbing back up to close above the day's opening price. This candle has formed at a key level, as part of an already established uptrend. I will make my entry at its close, 1.3035, with my stop loss at 1.2952 and a target at the previous November lows of 1.3231. This gives a nice risk-reward ratio on a high-probability trade.

Trade 8

Pair	EUR/USD
Order	1.3035 BUY
Stop loss	1.2952
Limit	1.3231
Risk	83
Reward	196

Wednesday, 25 January 2012

So much for high probability! I have been stopped out of yesterday's EUR/USD trade (Trade 8), for an 83 pip loss. A look at the chart in Figure 3.23 shows how.

FIGURE 3.23 - STOPPED OUT OF EUR/USD TRADE

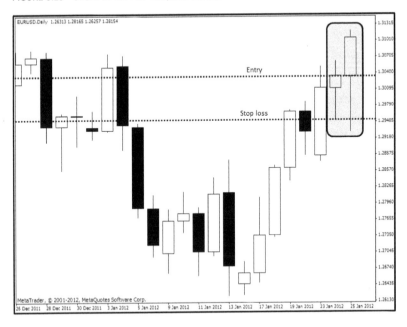

A frustrating stop-trigger, this one. Price has done as I suspected, following the pin bar with a close above the key resistance and a substantial gain on yesterday's levels. However, in doing so it first fell all the way to the low of the pin bar traded and broke through it, triggering the stop, before reversing. It would not surprise me if there is now a continuation in price movement up to the target I set, which would be very annoying.

On the bright side this gives me an opportunity to reinforce another important bit of discipline I apply in my trading. In this situation it is very tempting to look for a point to jump back into the trade and make back some of those losses. This comes from the feeling that the analysis was right, so the profit is deserved.

This is not so.

Profits are garnered from our analysis and our execution falling into line with how the market moves. If any of these three factors do not align then we lose the trade and move on. Some people like to buy into a losing trade on the premise that if their analysis is still correct then the price the market is trading at is a better one than they were presented with originally. Whilst mathematically this is logical, in my experience it serves to amplify losses more often than it serves to offset them, so I don't do it.

What does serve to offset losses in a stop trigger is a target hit on another trade (Trade 7, 24 January). A look at today's USD/JPY action in Figure 3.24 shows price breaking through my target at 78.19 for a gain of 88 pips.

FIGURE 3.24 – PROFIT TARGET HIT IN USD/JPY

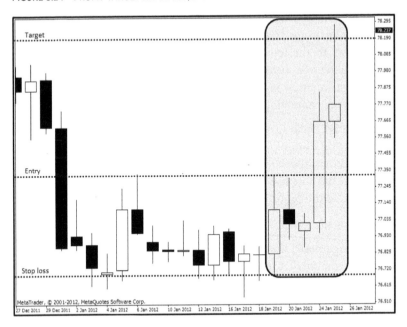

Whilst I might be tempted to consider myself unlucky in my EUR/USD trade, I think I can consider myself incredibly fortunate to have booked profits at the level I did in this one. You can see price moved rapidly towards the level at which I had predicted resistance might be found, but quickly reversed from that level to close just above its opening price.

This presents me with something of a dilemma. If I was to be shown this chart today, not having just traded successfully to the upside, my immediate bias would be towards the downside. A textbook pin has formed off strong resistance, with reward being offered all the way down at around 76.67. Emotionally this is a tough call to make, as it goes against the analysis on which I rested my margin yesterday.

As I have already covered, it is wise to avoid emotional decisions when it comes to trading and whilst this trade may *feel* wrong, by the rules of my strategy it presents a great opportunity.

Remember, I let my adherence to my rules dictate how I feel about a trade. This is a classic example. If I do take this trade and lose, I know it was based on sound principles. If however I do not take it and price does as my strategy suggests it should, then it will be an opportunity lost, a trade missed based on emotion, for which I could only blame myself.

With this in mind, I will let my strategy do the work on this one and enter the trade with my usual risk parameters, as outlined below.

Trade 9

Pair	USD/JPY
Order	77.75 SELL
Stop loss	78.27
Limit	76.67
Risk	52
Reward	108

Tuesday, 31 January 2012

That is the first month of the trading diary complete.

I will start my closing comments for the month on a positive note: my USD/JPY trade on 25 January (Trade 9) hit its target today, for a gain of 108 pips. If you remember, this was the emotionally difficult trade which called for a reversal in bias in what turned out to be a couple of hours.

A look over the entry that day suggests I was a little frantic in my decision making, but my conviction to hold fast to the rules of my strategy worked in my favour and once again my methods were vindicated.

Trade review for Month 1

So how did the month turn out? I will start with a summary of figures in Table 3.1.

Out of a total of nine trades placed, eight have closed and one is still open. I have not included the trade that is still open in the table of results for now, but I will do so when it closes.

TABLE 3.1 – SUMMARY OF MONTH 1 TRADES

Trades placed	9
Trades long	7
Trades short	2
Winning trades	6
Losing trades	2
Open trades	1
Profit (pips)	664
Loss (pips)	141
Overall profit/loss	523

From the eight closed trades I have come out with a profit of 523 pips. Whatever your account size, this is a substantial amount to gain in one month.

It should be noted that in terms of expected results, these are exceptional. The average win rate associated with my strategy is around 50:50, so I do not expect to maintain a win rate of six out of every eight trades over this entire diary period, but as a starting point I am extremely happy.

What I am even happier with is the way in which I have gone about gleaning such a profit from the market. Each of my trades has been subject to strict identification criteria and risk management rules, which I applied consistently throughout the period.

This is the part of trading that people find most difficult to grasp, but I genuinely believe that what I have taken from the market this month is not through careful, accurate analysis, but rather through risk management application. As this is the case, it suggests such profits can be gained by anybody who is in control of their emotions.

Overall, this was an excellent month's trading. Bring on February!

MONTH 2
Wednesday, 1 February 2012

After a strong performance in the first month of the year, I move into February with an air of caution about my trading. Historically, as I have mentioned before, the strategy I use normally runs profitably at a win rate of approximately 50%. What this means is that while 50% of my trades mature as winners, 50% of them are losers and hit their protective stops.

My win rate was 75% on my completed trades in January, with one trade still running. Surely a good thing I hear you say? Well, yes, on the one hand. On the other hand it suggests that to reconvene with the historical average over the past four years, a bad month should at some point present itself. In view of this, in February I will tighten up my risk parameters and I will not look to take any trades that present themselves as overly risky.

This situation also allows me to raise an interesting point. Many traders, perhaps some reading this, will consider this discretionary approach to trade identification to be an alteration of my strategy and in a sense this would be right.

Whilst I consider my strategy fundamentally to be a mechanical one, based on the fact that my trade identification and risk management are rules-based, there is an element of discretion between identification and execution.

If I am not happy with a trade, for whatever reason, I won't take it. This discretion is only developed through many hours of screen time and many trades placed. Those who are new to trading should stick to a mechanical system until they have developed a *feel* for the markets they are trading in.

Those who are in a position to apply a limited amount of discretion to their trading strategy should do so, especially if that discretion helps overcome any psychological reservations. In this instance, I am using discretion to reaffirm my faith in a strategy that suggests a short-term loss could be on the cards.

So, all that said, let's take a look at the major pairs as they enter the new month.

EUR/USD

What happened in January?

Figure 3.25 illustrates price action in January for EUR/USD.

FIGURE 3.25 – JANUARY'S ACTION IN EUR/USD

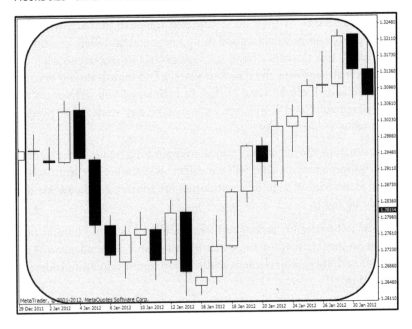

As you can see, in the first half of January the euro fell against the dollar, posting lows not seen since September of 2010. For the remainder of the month, there was a steep reversal from the low of 1.2623, with the pair completely recovering the lost ground by 24 January and continuing to rise thereafter. The month closed out around the key swing low of last November.

What might happen in February?

Although some consolidation should be expected following the steep uptrend witnessed last month, I feel that once this has taken place there may be a continuation of the trend. I will be on the lookout for candlestick patterns around the January highs to initiate a long trade. For the bias to become invalidated, I would need to see a strong series of closes below what has now become in-term support at around 1.3050.

AUD/USD

What happened in January?

Figure 3.26 illustrates the price action in January for AUD/USD.

FIGURE 3.26 – JANUARY'S ACTION IN AUD/USD

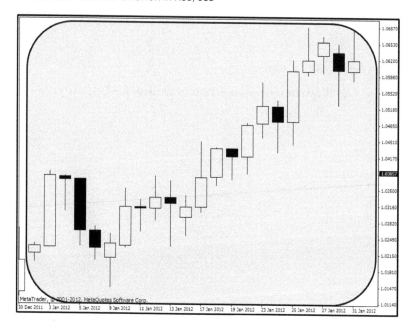

Despite a rocky first week or so, the Aussie dollar was able to reaffirm its predominant uptrend against its US counterpart, a rise that once in motion was to continue all the way through January. Price looks to still be moving upwards, but is very close to a key high at 1.0750. Looking at the action of the previous year tells me that this has been a key reversal point in the past.

What might happen in February?

Whilst the action seen over the past six weeks makes it hard to form any bias other than towards a continuation of the uptrend, I must consider the fact that the key level this pair is approaching has on a number of occasions turned this pair around. For a trend to break through a point of past price contention there often needs to be some form of catalyst. For example, a fundamental shift in perception surrounding the pair can be caused by the release of a piece of overly positive or negative data.

Whilst I am not in the business of interpreting data releases, their effect can be pivotal in providing the necessary fuel to break a technical boundary. Without this fuel, the pair may trade up to or at this level for a period, but may not be able to break and hold above it. Price action should give me the clue I need about what will happen.

USD/JPY

What happened in January?

Figure 3.27 illustrates the price action in January for USD/JPY.

FIGURE 3.27 - JANUARY'S ACTION IN USD/JPY

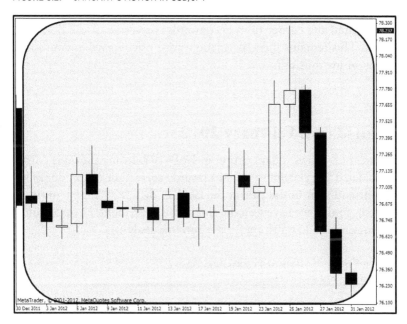

If you recall my first entry with regards to this pair last month, you will remember me saying it has a habit of extremely indecisive price action. January was no exception, with trading in a narrow range for nearly the whole month until a kick saw prices break both the upper resistance and then the lower support channels in the space of a week. I am still waiting for a trend to emerge before I form any bias on the direction of the pair.

What might happen in February?

Whilst no apparent trend is forming, there are a couple of things I am thinking about moving into February. The first of these is that over the past four to five years, USD/JPY has been in constant decline and – excluding the latter half of 2011 – is trading at an all-time low. The US dollar has never been so weak in relation to the Japanese yen. The second is that for the past six months or so price has been bouncing along at this level, breaking through a couple of times but without being able to sustain that break.

I try to avoid picking tops and bottoms, but the optimist in me feels like USD/JPY may have bottomed out in the last month and could be just around the corner from an upwards correction of the dominant trend. This remains pure speculation until price serves to confirm or discount my musings.

Thursday, 2 February 2012

Figure 3.28 shows today's action in USD/JPY. In my previous entry I considered the possibility of an upwards correction of the dominant downtrend seen in the pair in the last half decade. Whilst I am in no way suggesting we have seen the end of this movement, an opportunity has arisen for a low-risk trade based on this analysis.

FIGURE 3.28 – BULLISH PIN BAR FORMATION USD/JPY

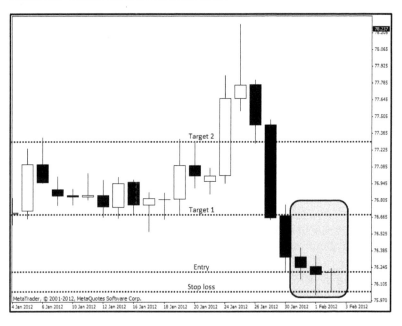

As you can see, price fell to a key low not seen since September/October 2011 and broke through it, but has failed to close below it, forming a small bullish pin bar in the process. A closer look at the action of the final day in January and yesterday reveals a further pattern forming, the *turnaround*. I described this pattern in Chapter 2 – it involves an inside day forming and then a break of the mother candle immediately followed by a return to within the mother candle's boundaries.

Both patterns – the bullish pin bar and the turnaround – forming at such a key low is too much of a tempter, so I will trade the setup as follows. My entry will be at the close of today's candle, 76.19, with my stop at the low of the same candle, 76.03. My initial target will be placed at the previous swing low of 76.67, with a secondary target of 77.28. This second target is based on the 77.28 level acting as resistance throughout January. If price does break through my initial target, it will likely encounter further resistance as it reaches this level. If my first target is met I will move my stop to breakeven at my entry price of 76.19 and see what happens.

This is inherently risky in that the chances of seeing a considerable correction off this low, as opposed to a break of it, are pretty slim. But the fact that the pattern has formed at key support and the candle has posted a small tail offers very attractive risk-reward parameters.

This attractive risk-reward has the effect of dulling the inherent risk of the trade because if I am right I stand to gain considerably and if I am wrong my loss will not be crippling and I can move on to another pair.

I will buy two lots, which will allow me to remove half of my position at the first profit target and half at the second if it is hit.

Trade 10

Pair	USD/JPY
Order	76.19 BUY (2 lots)
Stop loss	76.03
Limit	76.67/77.28
Risk	16 (x2)
Reward	48/109

Also today, my long trade in the Aussie dollar (Trade 6) has hit its target for a gain of 300 pips. This is shown in Figure 3.29.

FIGURE 3.29 – PROFIT TARGET HIT IN AUD/USD

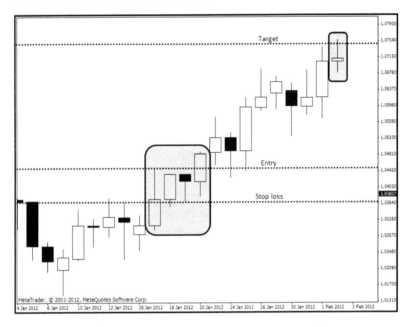

I placed this trade on 20 January, based on an inside candle formation.

Friday, 3 February 2012

There was very little definitive action from my three majors today, certainly nothing tradable. However there is something I would like to point out in EUR/USD as *one to watch*.

A look at the action towards the end of this week doesn't really give much away in terms of possible future direction, though it does serve to illustrate the indecision apparent in this pair. Prolonged indecision can lead to a substantial move and Wednesday's mother candle and the two inside candles immediately following, yesterday and today, really serve to illustrate this indecision. See Figure 3.30.

FIGURE 3.30 – INDECISION IN EUR/USD

I will keep an eye on this pattern, ideally looking for a break of the mother candle's upside limit to initiate a long trade that could continue last month's uptrend. A strong close above 1.3231 will further reinforce my bias.

Monday, 6 February 2012

A new week begins, another primary target hit! My trade on a short-term trend reversal in USD/JPY (Trade 10, 2 February) has paid off, with my primary target of 76.67 hit for a gain of 48 pips. See Figure 3.31.

FIGURE 3.31 – PROFIT TARGET HIT IN USD/JPY

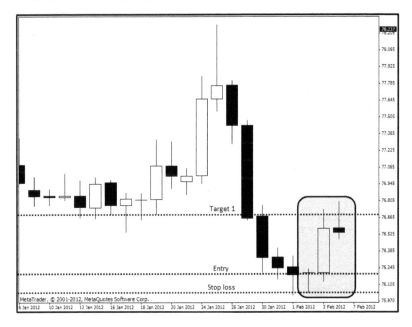

Although unable to close above the level, there could still be some way to go in terms of upwards movement. As per my trade outline I have moved my stop to breakeven and will leave this one to play out as either a stop at my entry or a profit take at my secondary target.

Also I'd like to revisit the EUR/USD chart I discussed towards the end of last week, as shown in Figure 3.32. As you can see yet another inside candle has formed, this time as a pin bar.

FIGURE 3.32 – MULTIPLE ENTRY SETUP IN EUR/USD

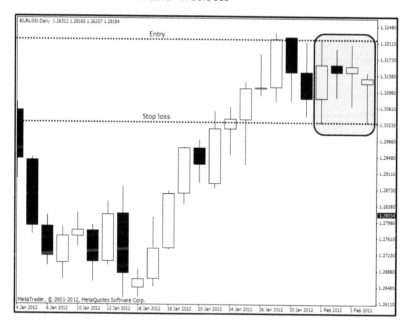

I have two options here. Entry at the close of this bar leaves me substantial upside if price can break through resistance at 1.3231 and continue up towards 1.3457. If I were to take this trade, my stop would be set at the pin bar's tail at 1.3027. What I am not convinced of is whether price would have enough momentum to break and hold above support once it has reached it and so it might not reach my target.

Alternatively, the high of the mother bar sits pretty much in line with resistance, just below 1.3231. If I was to wait until a break of this level before I entered, trading the inside day setup rather than the pin bar, I could be much more confident that price will break and hold above support.

Of course, this is a personal preference. Both look to be good setups, but in light of what I said at the start of the month regarding tight risk control I would rather wait. Perhaps I am missing an opportunity, but no money is ever lost through not taking a trade. I have set my entry at the high of the mother candle and as ever I will describe the trade if my order is filled.

Tuesday, 7 February 2012

Entry filled! A surge in price today, exactly what I was looking for, has resulted in my entry order being filled at the break of the pattern's mother bar, at 1.3218. This can be seen in Figure 3.33.

FIGURE 3.33 – ENTRY ORDER FILLED IN EUR/USD

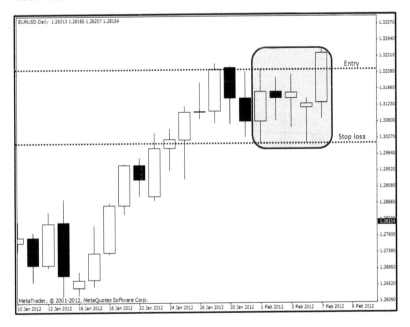

With today's price closing above the key support around 1.3231, I am looking for price to reach what has now become in-term resistance at around 1.3457.

Trade 11

Pair	EUR/USD
Order	1.3218 BUY
Stop loss	1.3025
Limit	1.3457
Risk	193
Reward	239

Thursday, 9 February 2012

There are a couple of things I would like to show you today.

The first of these is that my secondary target has been hit in my USD/JPY trade (Trade 10, 2 February), for a gain of 109 pips. This has resulted in a total gain for the trade of 157 pips. See Figure 3.34.

FIGURE 3.34 – PROFIT TARGET HIT IN USD/JPY

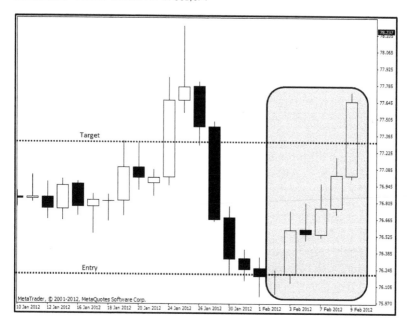

You might recall this trade was something of a punt, effectively relying on the price I bought at to become a bottom, requiring a short-term correction to see both targets hit. This is exactly what happened and it was another sound trade based purely on risk principles.

Second, have a look at the chart in Figure 3.35 showing today's AUD/USD price action.

FIGURE 3.35 – BULLISH PIN FORMATION IN AUD/USD

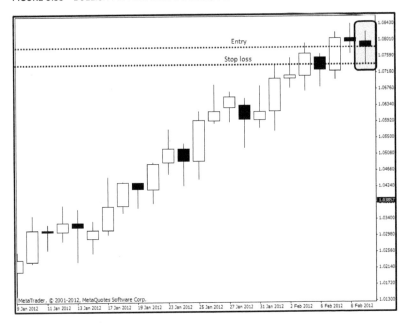

I can see a bullish pin candle has formed, with its tail piercing support at around 1.0753 and returning to close above. This suggests that there could be a continuation of last month's uptrend.

Whilst it is worth bearing in mind that price is close to all-time highs dating back to July 2011, if the support can hold there is still considerable upside from which to profit. The tail through support offers nice risk control and a target of 1.1000 – around those all-time highs I mentioned – provides me with a comfortable risk-reward ratio.

Trade 12

Pair	AUD/USD
Order	1.0786 BUY
Stop loss	1.0737
Limit	1.1000
Risk	49
Reward	214

Friday, 10 February 2012

As a trader quite often you have to hold up your hands and accept you were wrong. As a risk aware trader, hopefully when you are wrong it has not done too much damage to your account or your ego and so you are able to take it in your stride.

Today is one of those days for me. To start, I have been stopped out of yesterday's long AUD/USD trade (Trade 12) for a loss of 49. Whilst a controlled loss and very much absorbable, it is a particularly tough one as I had real confidence in the trade maturing as expected.

Looking at it from the other side, I have had a decent run in this pair of late and to give a small portion of what I have earned back is not too crushing. If you are one of those people that slow down when you pass a road traffic incident, the chart is shown in Figure 3.36.

FIGURE 3.36 – STOP LOSS HIT IN AUD/USD

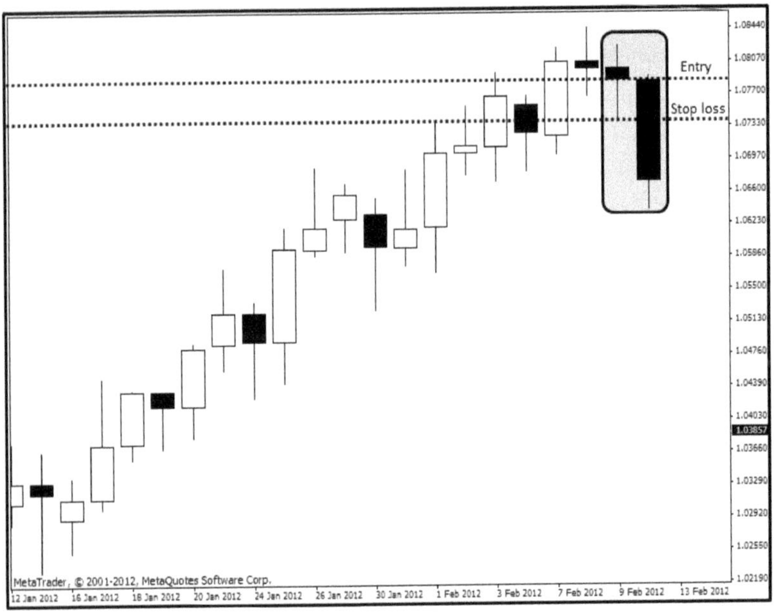

Having taken this loss, in hope of assuaging my grief I gravitated towards my other open trade to see if there was any reprieve to be had in EUR/USD (Trade 11). It seems that pair too has decided to turn around, closing below the key level I played for to the long side.

With neither target being hit, technically I shouldn't even be considering the outcome of this trade yet, but I felt I would mention it at the close of the week in the hope that come Monday my news can be decidedly more upbeat. I will write up the trade in the diary once it is complete. For now, bring on the weekend.

Wednesday, 15 February 2012

A slow start to the week has brought me to Wednesday with very little of note in terms of signals or possible setups. My EUR/USD trade (Trade 11) has continued to go against me; I fear it will soon look to test my stop at the lower end of the mother candle I traded from.

USD/JPY has continued to gain momentum in its upwards charge, so the call I made at the beginning of the month that there might be a short-term reversal is looking more and more to be a reality as each day passes. I am on the lookout for a point at which to rejoin the trend and will be watching closely as price approaches last October's highs at 79.52.

The reason for today's entry is an opportunity that has presented itself to the downside in AUD/USD. This is shown in Figure 3.37.

FIGURE 3.37 – BEARISH PIN FORMATION IN AUD/USD

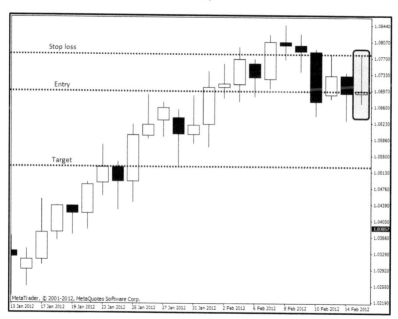

As you can see, a bearish pin has formed at resistance, suggesting a turn towards previous swing support at 1.0527. I have entered the trade at the close of today's candle, 1.0692, with risk defined by the upper end of the tail at 1.0775. The target is at previous swing support, offering an attractive reward.

Whilst there could be further consolidation in the pair before a directional bias is formed, today's pin suggests that price may not return above what can now be classed as resistance at 1.0753.

Trade 13

Pair	AUD/USD
Order	1.0692 SELL
Stop loss	1.0775
Limit	1.0527
Risk	83
Reward	165

Thursday, 16 February 2012

Another day, *lose* another dollar. I have been wiped out of my EUR/USD long (Trade 11) by today's action, which pierced support at 1.3050 then hit my stop at 1.3025 and reached as low as 1.2973 before closing out above all three of these levels, comfortably within the barriers of the original mother bar I spotted way back on 1 February. This can all be seen in Figure 3.38.

FIGURE 3.38 – A WICK-DOWN STOPS ME OUT OF EUR/USD

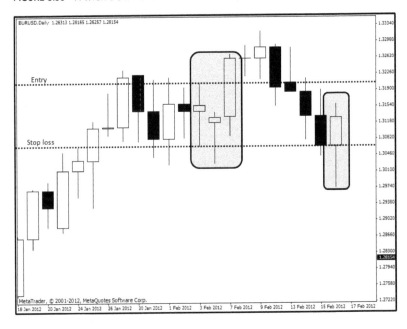

Whilst I must practice what I preach and not dwell on this loss, I would like to state my position. With price returning to close above the support level at which I positioned my stop, it would not surprise me if this pair flips back towards the upside, maybe even hitting the target I originally set.

Obviously I am out of the trade now, so it won't matter even if it does, but it is one to watch. What can happen – and what it looks like has happened in this instance – is when a pattern is formed at a key level, regardless of how other traders are identifying trades, you run the risk of placing your stop in line with the stops of other traders, in this instance just below support.

When price tests this level there is almost a domino effect that takes place, with sell order after sell order being filled as stop after stop is hit. This can serve to spike price downwards. If this is indeed what has occurred in this instance I would expect price to remain above its current level and continue its upside run towards my old target.

I like to think of this last paragraph as a valuable lesson to my readers. The bottom line is that I have taken a loss of 193 pips.

Friday, 17 February 2012

The bad news today is that another quick turnaround has seen another stop loss hit, this time in my AUD/USD trade (Trade 13). Figure 3.39 shows the pair struggling to carve out any obvious direction, bouncing up and down from the resistance at 1.0753. One such bounce proved fatal, closing out my trade for an 83 pip loss.

FIGURE 3.39 – STOPPED OUT OF AUD/USD

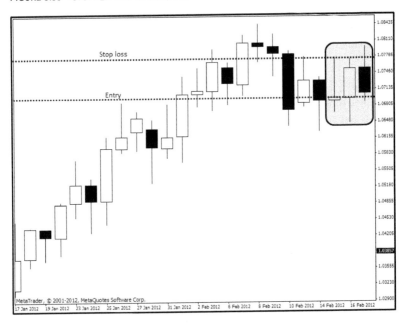

There is not too much to be said about this trade, other than I will continue to hold my downside bias in this pair, looking for any bearish candlestick patterns that could indicate some movement.

On a broader note, this week has been another tough one for me. A couple of trades I was really confident about have gone against me and for the second week running I have had to absorb some considerable losses.

Keeping me in the game is the fact that the losses I have taken have been controlled and therefore manageable, but psychologically it is becoming harder and harder to avoid jumping back into trades I have been stopped out of with the thought that price movement will eventually play out as I originally expected.

This is a cardinal sin when it comes to trading and is to be avoided at all costs, but even knowing this I can feel the temptation creeping in with each stop hit. This is a good example of just how hard it is to stay on top of your strategy psychologically.

Dark thoughts are unavoidable this evening. I hope to be able to write something more positive next week.

Tuesday, 21 February 2012

Take a look at the chart in Figure 3.40. It shows today's action in USD/JPY. Immediately noticeable is the uptrend the pair has carved out this month. I was lucky to have entered at the point I did way back on 2 February, as since then my strategy has signalled no other points of entry, until now.

FIGURE 3.40 - INSIDE DAY IN USD/JPY SUGGESTS CONTINUATION

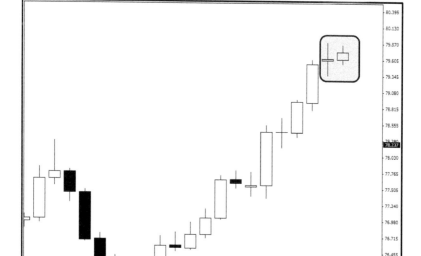

Today's action was contained well within yesterday's, forming an inside day. What makes it even more exciting is that it has formed almost to the pip at last October's highs of 79.53. Entry is on the break of the mother bar, at 79.89, with a key target at last July's high, 81.21. I have placed an entry order to this effect.

Risk can be derived from the lower end of the mother candle, 79.35. So long as the recent week's upwards momentum can be maintained, the target should be well within reach. I will enter the trade into my diary if my entry order is filled.

Wednesday, 22 February 2012

My entry was filled today, putting me long USD/JPY as per Figure 3.41.

FIGURE 3.41 – ENTRY ORDER FILLED IN USD/JPY

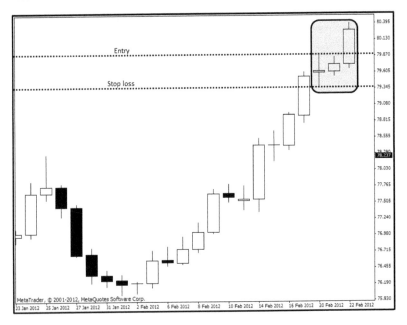

Trade 14

Pair	USD/JPY
Order	79.89 BUY
Stop loss	79.35
Limit	81.21
Risk	54
Reward	132

Another point of interest today can be seen in the EUR/USD chart in Figure 3.42.

FIGURE 3.42 – INSIDE DAY FORMATION IN EUR/USD

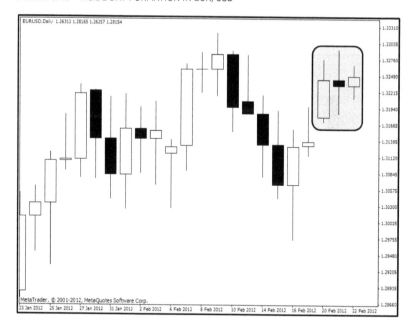

Comparison with yesterday's USD/JPY chart reveals an almost identical pattern forming, once again around a key level, suggesting that having bounced from last Thursday's low this pair could indeed be heading up towards the target I identified at the beginning of the month.

Entry would once again be triggered by a break of the mother bar at 1.3292, with December's key resistance forming a target. I place an entry order to this effect. Risk is set at the lower end of the mother candle's tail, 1.3186. As usual, if the entry order is filled I will then record the trade in the diary.

Thursday, 23 February 2012

And we're off! The entry in EUR/USD I described yesterday was triggered during today's price action, which is shown in Figure 3.43.

FIGURE 3.43 - ENTRY ORDER FILLED IN EUR/USD

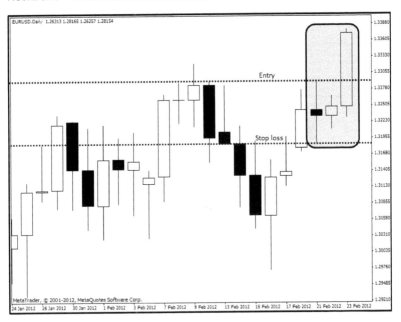

Trade 15

Pair	EUR/USD
Order	1.3292 BUY
Stop loss	1.3186
Limit	1.3460
Risk	106
Reward	168

I want to make an important point in relation to this trade. It is common to hear a trader brag about a particular winning trade they have placed, or a good trading month, etc. As a trader whose strategy relies upon a positive risk-reward ratio rather than a positive win-loss ratio, you can see how if I was to brag about a winner it would hold no bearing, or offer no insight as to my overall profitability in my trading operations.

Even less indicative of my overall trading results, but of considerably more weight when it comes to bragging rights, is my ability to hold out on this trade until now.

You will recall I was stopped out of this pair last week and when that happened I commented about a possible subsequent bounce from my stop loss position to the target I originally set. Convinced that this would be the case, I have watched this pair like a hawk each and every day, searching for a reason to go long. I have found a few, but none that have fallen in line with my strategy, so I did not act.

Today's trade is in my opinion vindication of my patience. As it has turned out, because I was patient an opportunity to enter has now presented itself that fits within the rules I apply to my trading. Whether this trade turns good or bad, as corny as it sounds, I feel like a winner.

Friday, 24 February 2012

Having risen quickly and substantially to put me into yesterday's EUR/USD trade (Trade 15), today's action has seen price do the same, this time taking me out of the trade for a gain of 168 pips. This is illustrated in Figure 3.44.

FIGURE 3.44 - PROFIT TARGET HIT IN EUR/USD

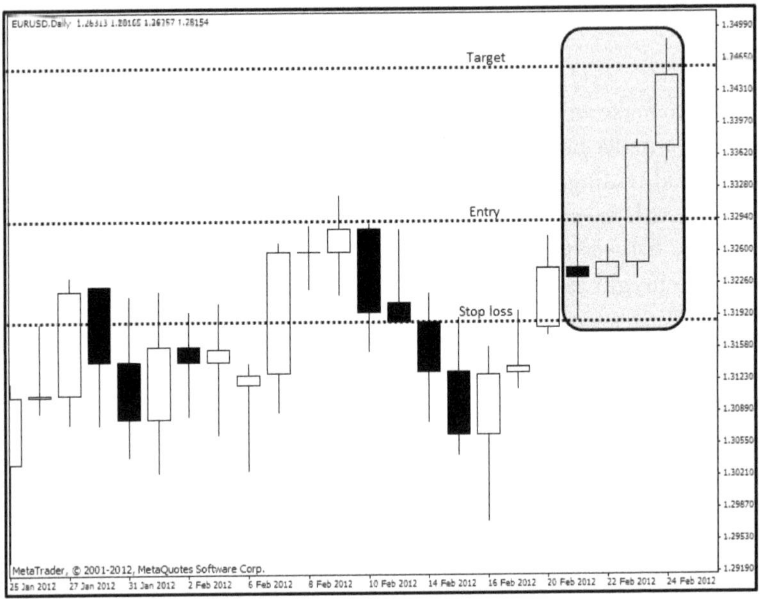

Sometimes a pattern serves to act exactly how I expect it to and this is one of those cases. As a side note, price has not closed above the resistance level seen in early December, suggesting that for now at least upwards progress could be halted.

Monday, 27 February 2012

Take a look at today's USD/JPY chart, shown in Figure 3.45.

FIGURE 3.45 – PROFIT TARGET HIT IN USD/JPY

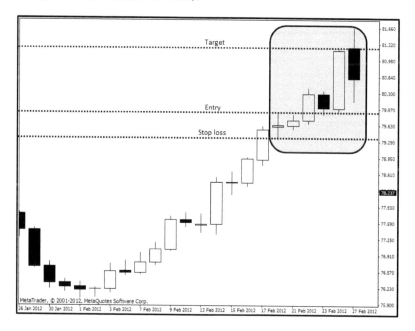

Having come within a pip of my target at 81.21 towards the end of last week, over the weekend I could not help but feel that I had misplaced my analysis and that come Monday this pair would turn around and go against me. As it happens, it was my worry that has turned out to be misplaced, with today's action seeing my profit target hit for a gain of 132 pips (Trade 14, 22 February).

Another textbook pattern produces another clean trade. After a tumultuous start to the month, it is reassuring both mentally and financially to see a couple of wins like this.

Tuesday, 28 February 2012

Today, once again, I am looking at the USD/JPY chart as shown in Figure 3.46.

FIGURE 3.46 – BULLISH PIN FORMATION IN USD/JPY

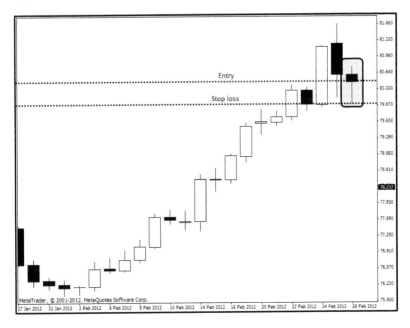

Having hit my target at 81.21 and closed out my trade yesterday, USD/JPY has fallen over the past two days, finding support around the 80.00 level, then towards the end of today it regained some of the losses to form a bullish pin bar.

Whilst continued momentum is required to break through in-term resistance, if it does I could look to the highs from May last year as a possible primary target. My stop loss is placed at the low of the candle, 80.01, and entry is at today's close of 80.44. Price has not been at this level for a while, so as mentioned I will look back to May last year to find a suitable target. The monthly swing high is at 81.94, which is a realistic target and offers suitable risk parameters.

Trade 16

Pair	USD/JPY
Order	80.44 BUY
Stop loss	80.01
Limit	81.94
Risk	43
Reward	150

Wednesday, 29 February 2012

It has been another patience-wrangler but on the last day of the month another opportunity has finally presented itself to go short AUD/USD.

Having been whipped around towards the end of last week, price has remained relatively confined within the channels of support/resistance surrounding 1.0750. A look at the chart (Figure 3.47) reveals a nice pin bar has formed at this level, offering attractive risk-reward for a move back down towards 1.0527.

FIGURE 3.47 – BEARISH PIN FORMATION IN AUD/USD

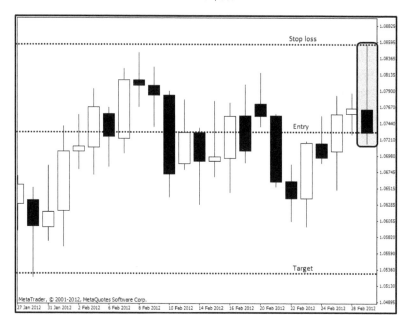

So with this target in mind, I place my stop loss at the pin bar high as usual and my entry is at the candle's close of 1.0729. This sees what looks to be my final trade of the month placed.

Trade 17

Pair	AUD/USD
Order	1.0729 SELL
Stop loss	1.0855
Limit	1.0527
Risk	126
Reward	202

Trade review for Month 2

Another month is at an end already. I close the week out with a couple of trades still open which, for the purposes of simplicity, I will not include in the month-end results for February and instead I will address them once they have closed.

In a similar vein, I began the month with an AUD/USD trade placed in January that closed on the second day of February. This trade is included in my summary figures for February. I should also note that my first trade of the month, which had two targets, has been logged as two separate trades, one per target hit.

A summary of my February trading is shown in Table 3.2.

TABLE 3.2 – SUMMARY OF MONTH 2 TRADES

Trades placed	8 (plus Trade 6, still open from 20 January)
Trades long	6
Trades short	2
Winning trades	4 (including Trade 6)
Losing trades	3
Open trades	2
Profit (pips)	757
Loss (pips)	325
Overall profit/loss	432

As far as bottom line is concerned, this is another great month. The big winner for me, against all my expectations, has been USD/JPY. USD strength took control of the pair and sent it on a steep upwards run, the biggest monthly advance seen since early 2010.

Luckily for me, the uptrend was indicated by a pin bar at the beginning of the month that enabled me to get on board. My targets were hit and having sat out of part of the advance, I was then given a second entry point indicated by an inside day, which enabled me to net more gains.

A couple of losers in AUD/USD and a particularly steep one in EUR/USD swallowed up some of what I made, but as stated towards the end of January, a gain of 400 to 500 pips in any one month is exceptional for my strategy so I can have no complaints.

As I have mentioned, it is often best not to dwell on losers and it is especially important to avoid thinking such things as "If I hadn't made that trade my profit would be higher," etc. The bottom line is the number we are left with when a strategy's signals are followed and the resulting profits or losses from trading these signals are reported. If you were to hypothetically alter the losing figures – saying "If I had done this…" and "If I hadn't done that…" – then your strategy would not be the same and thus the winning figures would change as well. As an evaluation method this would be futile.

Follow a strategy's rules to identify trades, make those trades using the strategy's risk management parameters and calculate results by subtracting pips lost from pips gained. Only once you have this bottom line figure can a strategy's performance be truly evaluated.

Onwards!

MONTH 3

Thursday, 1 March 2012

And so here we go again. As always I will start the month by considering what happened during last month's trading and how that might give me some indication of what to expect in the weeks to come.

EUR/USD

What happened in February?

Let's take a look at last month's chart, as shown in Figure 3.48.

FIGURE 3.48 – FEBRUARY'S ACTION IN EUR/USD

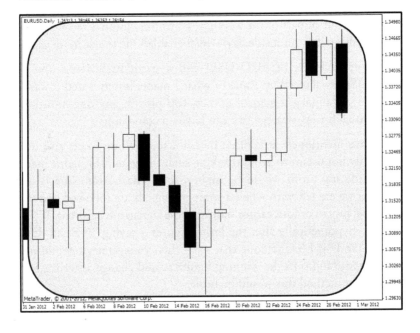

The chart shows that price action was range bound until 23 February when the pair broke through and closed above range resistance at around 1.3292. Reviewed in tandem with January's chart, I can see the pair has now been trading higher for two months – a strong upwards trend. However, I can also see the pair has reached a key resistance point dating back to December last year.

What might happen in March?

March could be a bumpy ride in this pair. In the medium term the advance throughout the beginning of this year could continue, but when reviewed in the context of the last year a strong overall downward trend combined with current price being at a key historic level makes me a little wary to buy into the pair just yet. If price action suggests short is the path of least resistance then that is where my money will fall.

AUD/USD

What happened in February?

Last month's chart is shown in Figure 3.49.

FIGURE 3.49 – FEBRUARY'S ACTION IN AUD/USD

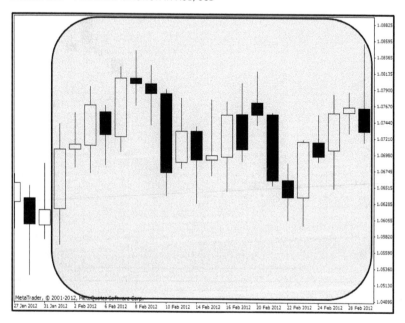

Having traded in a strong upwards direction throughout January, I mentioned at the beginning of last month that this pair could be set for a period of consolidation. A look at the chart suggests that this consolidation has occurred, with the pair trading sideways in a tight range throughout February. This is reflected in the signals generated and acted upon, with the sideways action making it very difficult to generate a profit.

What might happen in March?

This consolidation having taken place, I would now expect a trend to re-establish itself, with no general bias. As I write this I am short the pair, having taken a pin bar signal on the closing day of the month.

USD/JPY

What happened in February?

The month of February in USD/JPY is shown in Figure 3.50.

FIGURE 3.50 – FEBRUARY'S ACTION IN USD/JPY

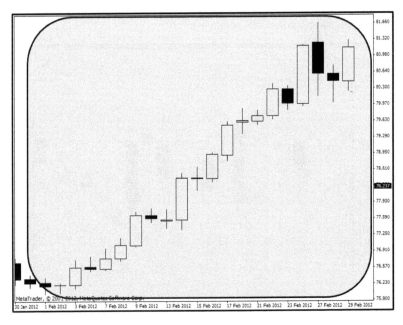

This was an ideal month in terms of following a trend. Established and signalled on the first day, the trend continued to generate entry points throughout, enabling me to take a good few pips from this pair.

What might happen in March?

The last few days of the month saw price swing considerably, which could indicate two things. The first is that a top has been reached, in which case there could be a period of consolidation similar to that which we saw in the Aussie dollar last month.

Alternatively, there might be a continuation. As I write this I am currently long the pair, having acted upon a pin bar signal on the last day of last month. If continuation is to occur then highs dating back to March 2011 could come into effect as targets.

* * *

Today, rather than write about a trade I made, I would like to point out instead one that I didn't. During the last few days of February EUR/USD posted a mother candle followed by two inside days and on the final day of the month the mother candle was broken to the downside, which according to my strategy should initiate a short. This action is shown in Figure 3.51.

FIGURE 3.51 – A MISSED OPPORTUNITY IN EUR/USD?

Through nothing other than my own incompetence, I did not see the setup forming and I missed the trade. Whilst I am sure another position will present itself, as I write this missed trade sits close to 100 pips from my hypothetical entry, which makes it hard not to be frustrated with myself. I will see if this missed opportunity is to cost me at the end of the month.

Monday, 5 March 2012

Take a look at the USD/JPY chart of today's action in Figure 3.52. I am already long this pair (Trade 16, 28 February), but price action towards the end of last week suggested that this uptrend could be set to continue, perhaps towards March 2011's high around 83.00.

FIGURE 3.52 – BULLISH PIN BAR FORMS IN USD/JPY

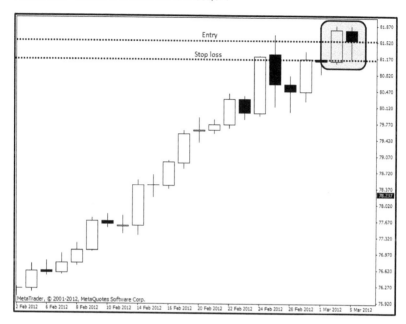

Action today has given me a reason to enter a new trade in the same pair. Price took a jump on Friday, with today's trading correcting a portion of that gain but picking up to close just below its opening level, forming a pin bar. My stop loss is at the low of the pin bar (81.15) and my target is just short of those March 2011 highs at 82.98.

Trade 18

Pair	USD/JPY
Order	81.54 BUY
Stop loss	81.15
Limit	82.98
Risk	39
Reward	144

Whilst I already have an active interest in USD/JPY, this new trade is based on a different signal to that which I entered on originally, so I will treat it as a completely separate trade.

Tuesday, 6 March 2012

I will start with the good news. Take a quick look at the AUD/USD chart in Figure 3.53.

FIGURE 3.53 – PROFIT TARGET HIT IN AUD/USD

As you can see, from the point at which I placed my short trade at the end of last month (Trade 17, 29 February), this pair has seen three consecutive days of falling prices. This has served to reach my profit target almost to the pip, for a gain of 202 pips. Another good AUD/USD trade to kick off the month.

Now for the bad news...

FIGURE 3.54 – STOPPED OUT OF USD/JPY

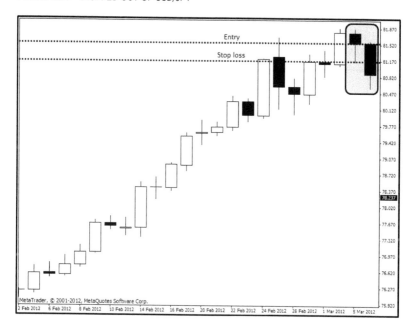

MetaTrader, © 2001-2012, MetaQuotes Software Corp.

As shown in Figure 3.54, the trade I placed yesterday in USD/JPY (Trade 18) has had its stop loss hit already, with a quick turnaround and decline in prices seeing the pair close below the support I have been working from for a couple of weeks now.

It is worth mentioning that I am still long this pair, with the trade I placed last month having neither its stop nor its target reached as of yet (Trade 16, 28 February). Whilst it is a shame to take a loss, I still feel confident that the pair can move up towards my original target, with my bias remaining long for the time being. As it stands I take a loss of 39 pips.

Wednesday, 7 March 2012

Having stopped me out of Monday's trade, USD/JPY has generated another signal today. After tumbling through support it seems to have found a foothold around 80.58 and has produced a pin bar candlestick suggesting continuation of the uptrend. This is shown in Figure 3.55.

FIGURE 3.55 – BULLISH PIN BAR/INSIDE DAY FORMATION IN USD/JPY

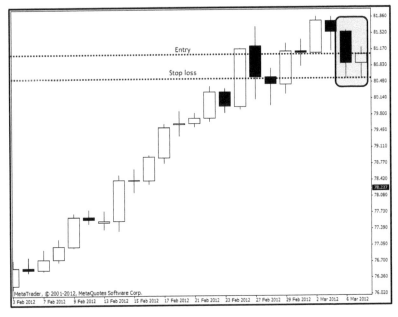

Despite my concerns that I am becoming somewhat emotionally attached to re-entering this pair long, I place another trade off this signal. My entry is at the pin bar's close, my stop loss is at the pin bar's low and my target is at the most recent swing high. Fingers crossed.

Trade 19

Pair	USD/JPY
Order	81.06 BUY
Stop loss	80.58
Limit	81.94
Risk	48
Reward	88

Friday, 9 March 2012

A couple of things are worth mentioning today. The first of these is a profit target hit in both of my open USD/JPY trades (Trade 16, 28 February and Trade 19, 7 March). Figure 3.56 illustrates the action that got me there.

FIGURE 3.56 – PROFIT TARGETS HIT IN USD/JPY

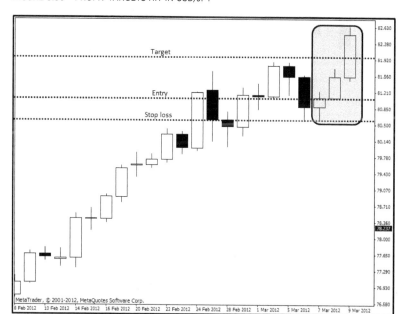

Three consecutive days of trading upwards saw price rocket towards the 82.00 level with my targets of 81.94 both being hit in the process. These are for gains of 150 pips and 88 pips respectively. There could still be more upside to go in this pair so I will continue to watch for candle patterns that might indicate good entry points.

The second topic of the day is a partially formed pattern in the Aussie. Take a look at the chart in Figure 3.57.

FIGURE 3.57 – INSIDE DAY FORMATION IN AUD/USD

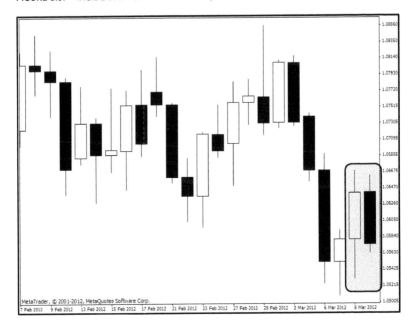

As you can see, price fell today to remain completely engulfed by yesterday's action. A break through the low of the mother candle could indicate a downside continuation, which if initiated could see price fall towards support at 1.0297. Risk-reward looks OK, with the mother bar's high capping my possible loss at 1.0669. I have placed an entry order to the short side, which I will outline in the diary as usual if it is filled.

Monday, 12 March 2012

Today's action (as shown in Figure 3.58) saw the order I placed to the downside on Friday being filled.

FIGURE 3.58 – ENTRY ORDER FILLED IN AUD/USD

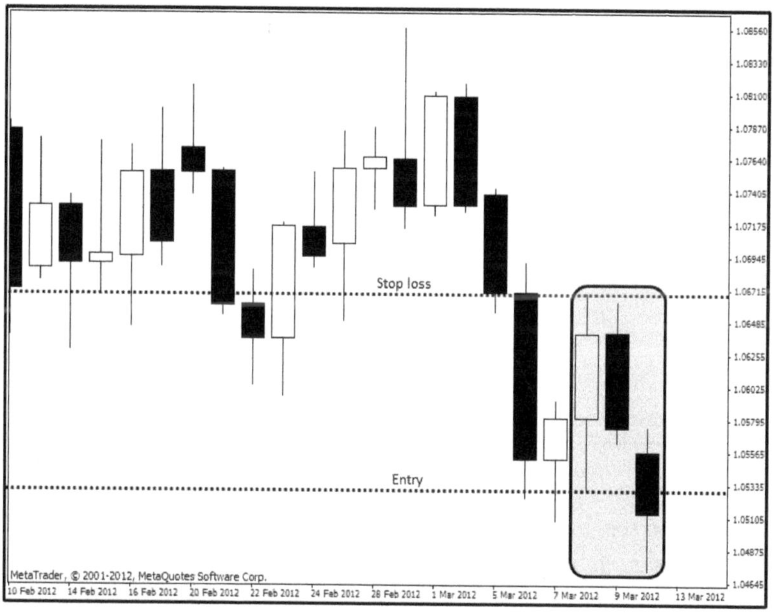

Trade 20

Pair	AUD/USD
Order	1.0522 Sell
Stop loss	1.0669
Limit	1.0297
Risk	147
Reward	225

Also of note today is an inside candle formed in USD/JPY, illustrated in Figure 3.59.

FIGURE 3.59 – INSIDE DAY FORMATION IN USD/JPY

As you can see, having risen for the majority of last week, price action today has seen the pair drop slightly, remaining well within the boundaries of Friday's candle. This inside day suggests a continuation of the extensive upwards run in the pair, possibly towards the highs seen in February last year. A break above Friday's high would see the pattern complete. I place an entry order at this level.

Tuesday, 13 March 2012

Entry order in USD/JPY filled (see Figure 3.60).

FIGURE 3.60 – ENTRY ORDER FILLED IN USD/JPY

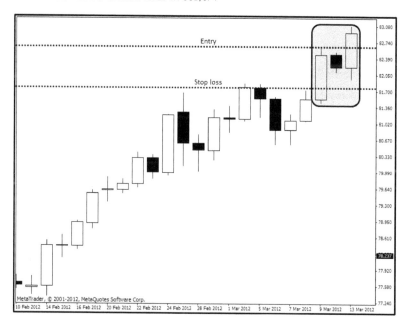

Trade 21

Pair	USD/JPY
Order	82.64 BUY
Stop loss	81.86
Limit	83.74
Risk	78
Reward	110

Notice that contrary to the pattern rules, I have used a level just below previous resistance (the assumption being it will now hold as support) as a stop level, instead of using the mother candle's low. The run in prices seen on Friday sees the low of the candle placed too far away from the current inside day to meet my risk-reward requirements. If this is the case then an alternative stop position is warranted providing it is supported technically. Previous levels of contention, as well as round numbers, can often provide this alternative.

Wednesday, 14 March 2012

Some of my favourite trades are those that offer a quick turnaround; trade identified, placed and target hit all within a few days. Trade 21 is an example of such a trade, with today's action seen in Figure 3.61.

FIGURE 3.61 – PROFIT TARGET HIT IN USD/JPY

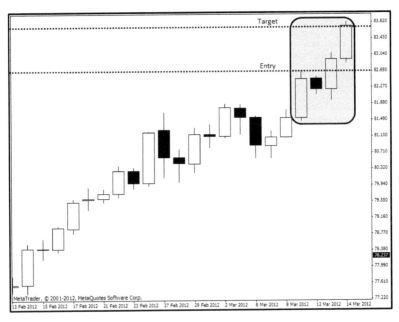

As you can see having filled my order and entered me into the trade, price continued to rally throughout Tuesday. Today presented much the same move, picking up where price left off last night to continue trading to the upside and hitting my target before returning to close just below it. A gain of 110 pips.

You may have noticed that a regular feature of my profit taking is seeing price hit my targets, then fall back to close below them on a daily basis. This is no coincidence. The fact that I use key historic price levels to pick my targets means that more often than not, when a target is hit – be it to the upside or the downside – the price at which it has been placed has acted as support or resistance in the past. These contentious levels replay themselves, giving the kick off of target prices that often occurs.

Taking this a step further, it can normally be assumed that if price breaks straight through a target then that particular price point is no longer a valid support or resistance level and trend continuation is implied.

Monday, 19 March 2012

Today's USD/JPY is shown in Figure 3.62.

FIGURE 3.62 – BULLISH PIN BAR SUGGESTS CONTINUATION IN USD/JPY

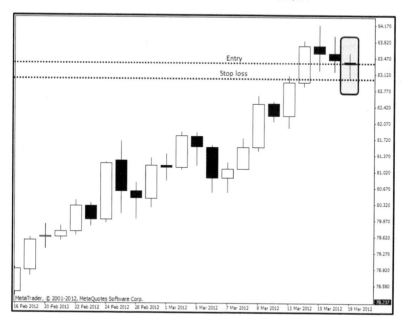

Since hitting my previous price target last Wednesday, this pair has been trading steadily downward towards key support. Today you can see that it has formed a pin bar, suggesting a further continuation of the overall uptrend is on the cards. Highs from November 2010 offer a nice upside, with the low of the pin bar's tail locking in risk.

Trade 22

Pair	USD/JPY
Order	83.33 BUY
Stop loss	83.01
Limit	84.29
Risk	32
Reward	96

Tuesday, 20 March 2012

Take a look at today's EUR/USD chart as shown in Figure 3.63. The run that carried the pair upwards towards the end of last week continued throughout yesterday, sending price towards a key historic resistance level at 1.3231.

FIGURE 3.63 – BULLISH PIN/INSIDE DAY IN EUR/USD

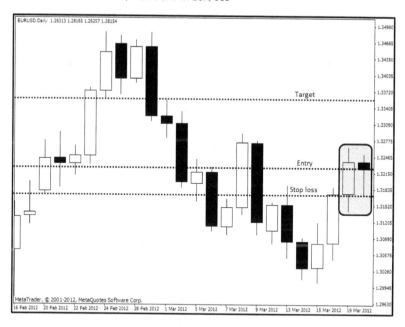

Today's action has seen a pin bar form, with price initially falling correctively before strengthening to close the day not far from its open. Entry is at today's close, with downside defined by the candle's tail and upside around near-term resistance at 1.3335.

Trade 23

Pair	EUR/USD
Order	1.3222 BUY
Stop loss	1.3171
Limit	1.3335
Risk	51
Reward	113

Thursday, 22 March 2012

What a day! I sat down at my computer this evening to assess the day's action and have been hit straightaway with two open trades being stopped out.

The first is in my EUR/USD trade from 20 March (Trade 23). The price action is shown in Figure 3.64.

FIGURE 3.64 – STOPPED OUT OF EUR/USD

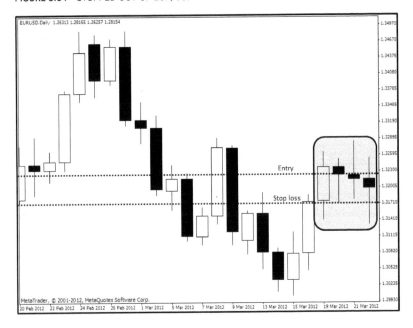

Having traded to the upside from the pin bar formed, price never really got going and has bounced around this level for the past couple of days, with today's action spiking down and taking out my stop loss. Interestingly enough, in doing so it has produced another buy signal, which I will cover in a moment. For now I have taken a 51 pip loss.

The second is my USD/JPY trade from 19 March (Trade 22). The price action is shown in Figure 3.65.

FIGURE 3.65 – STOPPED OUT OF USD/JPY

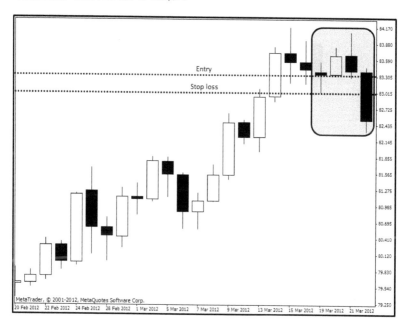

I had traded the bullish pin bar, looking for a target of 84.29 as taken from the November 2010 highs. Having initially looked promising, it seems my target was misplaced and turned out to be slightly out of reach for the pair. Having peaked at 84.17 price has now plummeted, taking out my stop in the process. Another loss, this time of 32 pips.

These losses aside, referring back to EUR/USD, today's action has formed a bullish pin bar at the same key level I traded from last time (shown in Figure 3.66).

FIGURE 3.66 – RE-ENTRY INTO EUR/USD

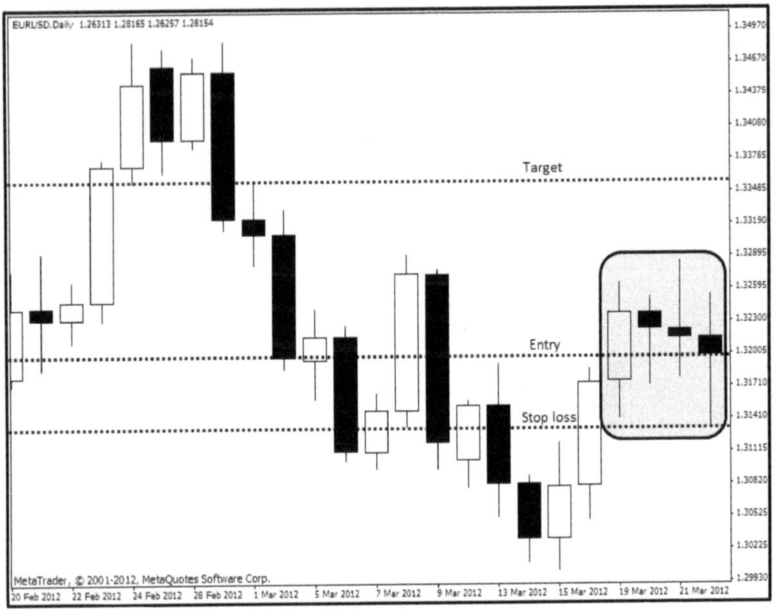

Last month I made a trade in this pair which a few days later was stopped out by a spike in prices and a few days after that the pair hit my original target. At the time I stated that if you get stopped out but still have faith in your original bias, do not jump back into the trade. Wait for another signal.

Here I am faced with exactly the same situation, the only difference being that the signal I would be looking to wait for has been produced today. From this, I can place another trade in same direction, with the same target and with slightly higher risk but an equally proportioned increase in upside available (as I am buying at a lower price). So here goes.

Trade 24

Pair	EUR/USD
Order	1.3199 BUY
Stop loss	1.3132
Limit	1.3335
Risk	67
Reward	136

Monday, 26 March 2012

Result! Have a look at the chart in Figure 3.67, showing today's EUR/USD action.

FIGURE 3.67 – PROFIT TARGET HIT IN EUR/USD

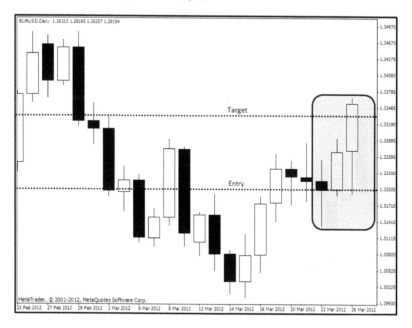

As you can see, since I went long this pair last Thursday (Trade 24) gains have been recorded throughout Friday and today, pushing price upwards and hitting my target at 1.3335 for a gain of 136 pips.

This is a good example of how important timing is in the market. The first trade I took towards this target was stopped out but the second hit, with the only difference between the two positions being a couple of days' worth of trading.

Thursday, 29 March 2012

The end of the month is approaching already!

A bit of a tumultuous one in terms of signal reliability and though I haven't totalled up the figures yet I suspect my bottom line will not be quite as strong as it was in January and February. Pessimism aside, a target has been hit, and two of the major pairs have produced very similar signals today.

First, the hit target. My long standing AUD/USD short from 12 March (Trade 20) has closed out for a nice gain of 225 pips.

Now for the signals.

The first is in EUR/USD (see Figure 3.68).

FIGURE 3.68 – BULLISH PIN BAR FORMATION IN EUR/USD

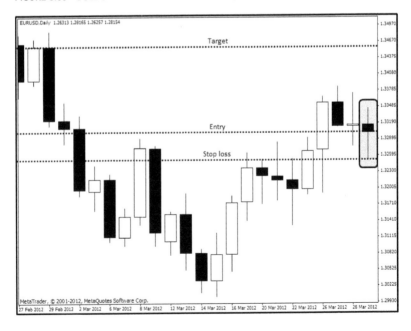

As you can see the euro has been strengthening steadily against its US counterpart since the middle of this month and has now reached an area that has acted as range resistance in the past. Today's action has seen the formation of a bullish pin bar, which could indicate further upside towards 1.3547, as seen at the end of last month. Entry is at today's close with the tail providing risk as always and a target as mentioned.

Trade 25

Pair	EUR/USD
Order	1.3301 BUY
Stop loss	1.3251
Limit	1.3457
Risk	50
Reward	156

The second signal for today can be seen in the AUD/USD chart in Figure 3.69.

FIGURE 3.69 – BULLISH PIN AT KEY SUPPORT IN AUD/USD

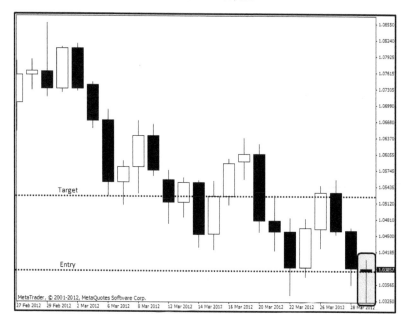

Whilst price has been steadily declining in this pair, it has reached key support at 1.0297 with today's action. This pair has seen some monstrous corrective waves over the past few years and if I am to believe that what I have seen this month is one such correction then this key level is as good as any for a turn back towards the upside.

Whilst I don't like to attempt to pick tops or bottoms, if price action at a key level supports a bias and if the risk-reward parameters are acceptable then I will trade what I see. As usual with a bullish pin bar, entry is at its close, the stop loss is at its low and my target is at a recent point of resistance.

Trade 26

Pair	AUD/USD
Order	1.0379 BUY
Stop loss	1.0303
Limit	1.0527
Risk	76
Reward	148

Friday, 30 March 2012

Another month of trading is complete. An excellent start to the year has left me anticipating a month of crushing trades which, seemingly, is still to come.

Review of Month 3

The figures for March are summarised in Table 3.3.

TABLE 3.3 – SUMMARY OF MONTH 3 TRADES

Trades placed	9 (plus Trade 16 and Trade 17 still open from 28/29 February)
Trades long	8
Trades short	1
Winning trades	6 (including Trade 16 and Trade 17 from February)
Losing trades	3
Open trades	2
Profit (pips)	911
Loss (pips)	122
Overall profit/loss	789

Amazingly, I have once again achieved a large profit – of 789 pips – in this month of trading. I will add the caveat that my results are bolstered by the two February trades closing in at a profit at the beginning of the month and there are also currently two trades with a fate yet to be decided, but as it stands this is another great month.

The conditions in which I am trading at the moment seem to be perfectly suited to the strategy I am using. This of course is not going to be the case throughout a trading career, but it is nice to get a few good months under my belt, especially in light of using my trades for the last three months as the basis for this book.

Something that you will learn throughout your career as a forex trader is that more often than not a year's figures can be broken down into *some losers, some winners* and *some big winners.*

The *some winners* are those months you posted gains and the *some losers* are those months you posted losses. More often than not these two categories will cancel each other out. It is the *some big winners* category that writes your bottom line figure.

The three months I have just traded fall well within the *some big winners* category, which whilst far from guaranteeing a big year, suggests that so long as I control my risk and do not allow a new category to be formed, namely *some big losers*, then I have a strong chance of positive annual returns.

Chapter Four

Analysis of Diary Period

This chapter can be considered a sort of post-match analysis. While I covered a lot of the trades in detail during the three months, I often gain a different perspective on my trading when I step back and take a look at it on aggregate. With this post-match analysis I hope to gain that perspective and present it to you.

Unresolved trades from the diary

Before I comment on the performance of my strategy throughout the first three months of this year there are a couple of unresolved trades I must address as these were still open when I completed my final diary entry.

The first of these was my long trade off the pin bar formed in AUD/USD on 29 March (Trade 26). On 4 April this trade was stopped out for a loss of 76 pips, as you can see in Figure 4.1.

FIGURE 4.1 – STOPPED OUT OF AUD/USD

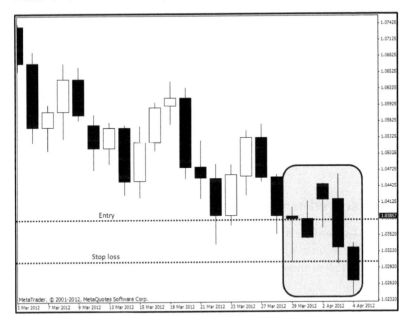

The second saw another stop hit in my EUR/USD trade from 29 March (Trade 25), as shown in Figure 4.2. The loss on this trade was 50 pips.

FIGURE 4.2 – ANOTHER STOP HIT, THIS TIME IN EUR/USD

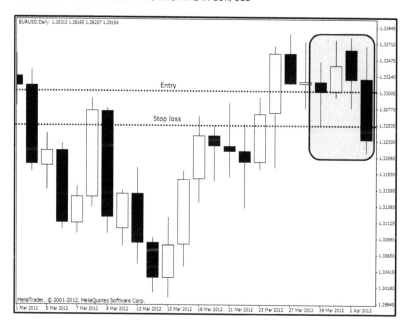

Alteration of the month's results to incorporate these two small losses leaves me with a total pip profit for March's trades of 663 pips.

Analysing my strategy during the diary period

Having addressed this, I will now consider the effectiveness of my strategy throughout the period based on three criteria:

1. Profitability
2. Signal generation
3. Tradability

1. Profitability

In terms of profitability, the price action strategy I put into effect over the first three months of 2012 returned a little more than 1600 pips in profit. By any standards this is a considerable gain.

Whilst I will not lay claim to this strategy producing this sort of return every month, my results show that by adhering to strict risk management rules it is possible to control losses so that they do not have too much of a deteriorative effect on the bottom line. Below is a summary of the three-month period.

TRADING SUMMARY OF THE FULL THREE-MONTH DIARY PERIOD

Total trades placed	26
Trades long	21
Trades short	5
Winners	16
Losers	10
Total pips lost	714
Total pips gained	2332
Overall profit/loss	**1618**

The win rate over the three months – that is the number of trades that produced a profit in relation to the number of trades that produced a loss – was somewhere in the region of 3:5. This is slightly more in favour of winning trades than historical trading under the same strategy.

The reality is that with the hard and fast rules of my strategy, and the constant ebb and flow of market conditions, a method will produce varying results when analysed in the short term. What is important is the long-term results.

What I mean by this is that if the first three months of 2012 had produced losses, rather than altering my strategy rules to fit the market conditions I would have made the assumption that the market conditions at that time were temporarily out of line with my methods. That would suggest to me that the next period would be in line, so the losses should be absorbed and I should continue to adhere to my rules. I know this is the right thing to do because I have traded this strategy for four years and I have seen results average out over time.

2. Signal generation

The second focus point in my analysis is signal generation. By this I mean how well my strategy responded to trend formation; did it signal entry? Also built into this point is the accuracy of the targets I followed and the stop losses I placed.

Over the course of the three-month period, my strategy signalled approximately nine or ten valid entries a month. I use the word *valid*, as there were entries signalled that I did not take due to excessive risk offered.

In terms of the way I like to approach the markets, I see this as ideal. As you have probably gleaned by now, whilst I take my trading very seriously, my approach to the market is somewhat relaxed. I don't like to clutter my charts with indicators, I usually only analyse the markets at the New York close and I only ever trade off daily charts. Around nine trades a month is just right for me and I am pleased with the signal generation of my strategy over the diary period.

The other side of my strategy's signalling ability is the accuracy in limit order and stop loss placement. A strategy that gets every signal correct is useless unless it also indicates where the pair should reach or the point at which the signal becomes invalid. It is vital to have these two factors built into any approach – some would argue it is even more important than the entry itself.

Over the three months traded I was very happy with the profit target placement suggested by my rules. My profit targets invariably come from levels of contention in historic price action. What you will have noticed throughout the live trading is that these levels are all previous support or resistance, more often than not the level that the pair I am trading is likely to encounter next.

The accuracy in this method was illustrated over the period by a number of trades in which the profit target placed was hit to within a few pips, before the pair reversed away from the key level. This reversal from my targets is something that has been a recurring event throughout the life of my strategy and for me it is the best indication there is that my target placement is correct.

If my trades were to consistently run 50 to 100 pips past my target, I could be excused for feeling sold short and a placement rethink might be in order as I could be missing out on gains with every trade. Conversely if I was falling short of my targets regularly, I could assume that I was being too greedy, chasing targets that weren't there and in response I could consider reducing my profit target on each trade.

The last thing to consider under the signal generation is the risk management conditions implied by each signal. The risk I take on each trade is indicated by and housed entirely within each pattern I use. For example, in a pin bar trade the risk is outlined by the pin bar's tail. This enables me to quickly and accurately decide whether a trade is an opportunity or not. Overall I am happy with the risk parameters my strategy presented over the period.

Over the course of the trading period, there were a couple of losses that I would consider to be on the upper end of what my strategy will tolerate. What I mean by this is that when it comes to trading daily candlesticks, I think very carefully before taking a trade that risks any amount of pips outside of double figures. Whilst I do take these trades, they are often on a discretionary basis. Of the 26 trades I placed during the period, four had triple figure risk associated with them.

The simple reason behind my reluctance to take these trades with very high risk is that I try to maintain as close to a one-to-two risk-reward ratio as possible. Depending on the volatility of the pair in question, it is rare to be able to say with confidence that I expect a profit target of, say, 250 to 300 pips to be reached. This would be the concomitant reward necessary for a trade with a risk of 125 to 150 pips.

Therefore it is rare that taking on a risk of over 100 pips can be justified. This is not to say that it should not be done – you will have seen that I made a number of plays for 200 to 300 pips in the diary period – but I am always cautious in doing so.

3. Tradability

Finally I come to the tradability of my strategy. What I mean by tradability is the ease with which I was able to recognise signals and in turn execute trades according to the rules I set.

I trade a very small number of patterns and I have become adept at recognising them very quickly if they appear. With my personal approach this recognition is made even easier by the fact that I trade daily charts, so I am under no time pressure to identify and trade quickly, which could lead to rash decisions.

This does not mean however that I never miss a trade; you will recall the setup I missed at the beginning of March in EUR/USD.

The tradability of my strategy is also increased by the strict rules it entails. The only part of the entire strategy that is discretionary is in deciding whether the risk-reward ratio on offer is sufficient to justify the trade. Even this is subject to a strict positive ratio, which I nearly always want to be close to or better than one-to-two.

The fact that the patterns I trade each have predetermined risk parameters makes it very easy for me to stick to the rules I set for myself. I would say that overall tradability of my strategy is something that I am happy with and its rules are something that I feel I could continue to implement throughout my trading career. Any beginner trader should develop a strategy about which they could say, and do, the same.

Chapter Five

Conclusion

I would like to take this opportunity to make some closing remarks about my strategy, myself as a trader and the forex market in general. Although I constantly analyse my own performance and my strategy's performance, this is the first time I have issued such detailed commentary on every trade I have taken in a period and my reasons for doing so.

I feel that taking such an approach has allowed me an objective perspective on my strategy, one which I probably would not have been able to achieve otherwise. Although I consider trading my profession, in that this is what I do to make money, I by no means consider myself an expert in the field. I believe that as traders we learn every single day and a constant evolution in the approach we take to any market is required if consistent, long-term profitability is to be achieved.

The rules of my strategy may not be as effective next year or the year after that. All I can say for certain is that in current market conditions, and under the conditions of markets past, I can trade effectively. I am willing and open to altering my approach, but only if the market suggests I should over an extended period. Anybody can trade foreign exchange, nearly anybody can make some money, but it is those who can ride the waves of losing and winning over the long-term that can consider themselves professional traders.

The methods described in this book are intended to illustrate how a simple, effective approach that is governed in its entirety by risk management principles can be implemented to good effect across a number of the major currency pairs. I do not intend to imply that by following my rules, anybody can become a professional currency trader. Far from it.

Automated trading?

Having read my diary some might put forward the argument that the patterns I trade could easily be written into a language that a computer would understand (MQL for example) and then I could sit back and let my platform trade for me while I found better and more enjoyable ways to spend my time.

However, first off, I enjoy trading and wouldn't really consider spending my time doing anything else. Second, and more importantly, those of you with a keen eye will have recognised that although I follow strict rules and trade the same patterns over and over, with the same risk parameters and targeting rules, there is an element of discretion in the way I approach the markets. When a trade is signalled I can decide which approach might suit the current market conditions best and trade accordingly.

Third, and finally, however consistent a strategy is, it will always require alterations to stay in line with what the market is doing. If I was to hand over the control of my strategy to a computer I would also be handing over the control I have in being able to recognise which elements of the market are changing and how I should adapt my strategy to suit. A financial market – and therefore trading in a financial market – is dynamic. Things change quickly and you have to adapt or get left behind.

Risk management + screen time

All too often I hear or read about the next big strategy, the Holy Grail that can turn a nine-till-five desk jobber into a work-from-home trader. Until people realise that these solutions do not exist, there will always be a negative light shone on the marketeers of the trading industry.

What is important as traders just starting out is to differentiate between these marketeers and those who offer genuine advice. Often an easy way to make this distinction is to see which of the so-called traders that are offering advice are charging for it. I have seen educational programmes ranging from a couple of hundred pounds up to thousands of pounds and each time a new one presents itself consider this – what are you getting for your money?

All of the education a trader needs can be developed through gaining a good grasp of risk management principles and by clocking up many, many hours of screen time. Screen time allows you to develop a sense of how the market moves and risk management principles allow you to stay active as a trader long enough for this sense to develop.

These two ingredients alone will offer more of a return than even the most expensive educational package available and they are both free.

Useful resources

Books

Robert Fischer, *Candlesticks, Fibonacci and Chart Pattern Trading Tools*
These are not really the patterns I trade, but there are some great descriptions of how price patterns develop that you can take into your own trading.

Robert Edwards and John Magee, *Technical Analysis of Stock Trends*
These are not really the patterns I trade myself, but this is a great way to learn about the fundamentals behind price action and pattern formation.

Steve Nison, *Japanese Candlestick Charting Techniques*
One of my all-time favourites and a great introduction to candlesticks.

Websites

www.forexfactory.com – A great place to interact with other traders.

www.investing.com – A source for staying on top of any news that might affect the pairs you are trading.

www.tradimo.com – A nice introduction to Forex, along with videos, quizzes and lessons to get you trading.

Appendix

FIGURE A – EUR/USD IN 2011

FIGURE B – AUD/USD IN 2011

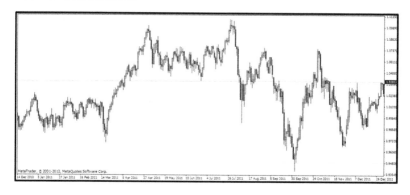

FIGURE C – USD/JPY IN 2011

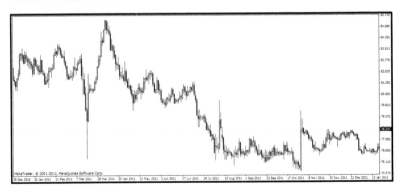